MznLnx

Missing Links Exam Preps

Exam Prep for

Business, Government, and Society: A Managerial Perspective

Steiner, 11th Edition

The MznLnx Exam Prep is your link from the texbook and lecture to your exams.
The MznLnx Exam Preps are unauthorized and comprehensive reviews of your textbooks.

All material provided by MznLnx and Rico Publications (c) 2010
Textbook publishers and textbook authors do not particpate in or contribute to these reviews.

MznLnx

Rico Publications

Exam Prep for Business, Government, and Society: A Managerial Perspective
11th Edition
Steiner

Publisher: Raymond Houge
Assistant Editor: Michael Rouger
Text and Cover Designer: Lisa Buckner
Marketing Manager: Sara Swagger
Project Manager, Editorial Production: Jerry Emerson
Art Director: Vernon Lowerui

Product Manager: Dave Mason
Editorial Assitant: Rachel Guzmanji
Pedagogy: Debra Long
Cover Image: Jim Reed/Getty Images
Text and Cover Printer: City Printing, Inc.
Compositor: Media Mix, Inc.

(c) 2010 Rico Publications
ALL RIGHTS RESERVED. No part of this work covered by the copyright may be reproduced or used in any form or by an means--graphic, electronic, or mechanical, including photocopying, recording, taping, Web distribution, information storage, and retrieval systems, or in any other manner--without the written permission of the publisher.

Printed in the United States
ISBN:

For more information about our products, contact us at:
Dave.Mason@RicoPublications.com

For permission to use material from this text or product, submit a request online to:
Dave.Mason@RicoPublications.com

Contents

CHAPTER 1
The Study of Business, Government, and Society — 1

CHAPTER 2
The Dynamic Environment — 3

CHAPTER 3
Business Power — 6

CHAPTER 4
Critics of Business — 8

CHAPTER 5
Corporate Social Responsibility — 13

CHAPTER 6
Implementing Social Responsibility — 18

CHAPTER 7
Business Ethics — 23

CHAPTER 8
Making Ethical Decisions in Business — 27

CHAPTER 9
Business in Politics — 29

CHAPTER 10
Federal Regulation of Business — 33

CHAPTER 11
Reforming Regulation — 40

CHAPTER 12
Multinational Corporations and Trade — 46

CHAPTER 13
Globalization — 50

CHAPTER 14
Industrial Pollution and Environmental Policy — 54

CHAPTER 15
Managing Environmental Quality — 58

CHAPTER 16
Consumerism — 63

CHAPTER 17
The Changing Workplace — 70

CHAPTER 18
Civil Rights at Work 544 19 Corporate Governance — 83

ANSWER KEY — 87

TO THE STUDENT

COMPREHENSIVE

The *MznLnx* Exam Prep series is designed to help you pass your exams. Editors at MznLnx review your textbooks and then prepare these practice exams to help you master the textbook material. Unlike study guides, workbooks, and practice tests provided by the texbook publisher and textbook authors, *MznLnx* gives you **all** of the material in each chapter in exam form, not just samples, so you can be sure to nail your exam.

MECHANICAL

The MznLnx Exam Prep series creates exams that will help you learn the subject matter as well as test you on your understanding. Each question is designed to help you master the concept. Just working through the exams, you gain an understanding of the subject--its a simple mechanical process that produces success.

INTEGRATED STUDY GUIDE AND REVIEW

MznLnx is not just a set of exams designed to test you, its also a comprehensive review of the subject content. Each exam question is also a review of the concept, making sure that you will get the answer correct without having to go to other sources of material. You learn as you go! Its the easiest way to pass an exam.

HUMOR

Studying can be tedious and dry. MznLnx's instructional design includes moderate humor within the exam questions on occassion, to break the tedium and revitalize the brain

Chapter 1. The Study of Business, Government, and Society

1. The _____ requires the Federal government to investigate and pursue trusts, companies and organizations suspected of violating the Act. It was the first United States Federal statute to limit cartels and monopolies, and today still forms the basis for most antitrust litigation by the federal government.
   a. 28-hour day
   b. 33 Strategies of War
   c. Sherman Antitrust Act
   d. 1990 Clean Air Act

2. _____ is an economic and social system in which trade and industry are privately controlled for profit. The means of production, which is otherwise known as capital and includes land are owned, operated, and traded for the purpose of generating profits, without force or fraud, by private individuals either singly or jointly. Investments, distribution, income, production, pricing and supply of goods, commodities and services are determined by voluntary private decision in _____, which is also known as a market economy.
   a. Adam Smith
   b. Affiliation
   c. Abraham Harold Maslow
   d. Capitalism

3. _____ was a writer, management consultant, and self-described 'social ecologist.' Widely considered to be 'the father of modern management,' his 39 books and countless scholarly and popular articles explored how humans are organized across all sectors of society--in business, government and the nonprofit world. His writings have predicted many of the major developments of the late twentieth century, including privatization and decentralization; the rise of Japan to economic world power; the decisive importance of marketing; and the emergence of the information society with its necessity of lifelong learning. In 1959, Drucker coined the term 'knowledge worker' and later in his life considered knowledge work productivity to be the next frontier of management.
   a. Debora L. Spar
   b. Jacques Al-Salawat Nasruddin Nasser
   c. Peter Ferdinand Drucker
   d. Chrissie Hynde

4. _____ was a German philosopher, political economist, historian, political theorist, sociologist, communist and revolutionary credited as the founder of communism.

Marx summarized his approach to history and politics in the opening line of the first chapter of The Communist Manifesto : 'The history of all hitherto existing society is the history of class struggles.' Marx argued that capitalism, like previous socioeconomic systems, will produce internal tensions which will lead to its destruction. Just as capitalism replaced feudalism, socialism will in its turn replace capitalism and lead to a stateless, classless society called pure communism which will emerge after a transitional period, the 'dictatorship of the proletariat', a period sometimes referred to as the 'workers state' or 'workers' democracy' .

a. Abraham Harold Maslow
b. Karl Heinrich Marx
c. Adam Smith
d. Marxism

5. _____ was a Scottish moral philosopher and a pioneer of political economy. One of the key figures of the Scottish Enlightenment, Smith is the author of The Theory of Moral Sentiments and An Inquiry into the Nature and Causes of the Wealth of Nations. The latter, usually abbreviated as The Wealth of Nations, is considered his magnum opus and the first modern work of economics.
a. Adam Smith
b. Abraham Harold Maslow
c. Affirmative action
d. Affiliation

6. _____ is a term used to describe a policy of allowing events to take their own course. The term is a French phrase literally meaning 'let do'. It is a doctrine that states that government generally should not intervene in the marketplace.
a. Laissez-faire
b. Freedom of contract
c. Deep ecology
d. Libertarian

Chapter 2. The Dynamic Environment

1. _____ in its literal sense is the process of transformation of local or regional phenomena into global ones. It can be described as a process by which the people of the world are unified into a single society and function together.

This process is a combination of economic, technological, sociocultural and political forces.

   a. Cost Management
   b. Histogram
   c. Collaborative Planning, Forecasting and Replenishment
   d. Globalization

2. The _____ was a period in the late 18th and early 19th centuries when major changes in agriculture, manufacturing, mining, and transportation had a profound effect on the socioeconomic and cultural conditions in Britain. The changes subsequently spread throughout Europe, North America, and eventually the world. The onset of the _____ marked a major turning point in human society; almost every aspect of daily life was eventually influenced in some way.

   a. Abraham Harold Maslow
   b. Affiliation
   c. Industrial revolution
   d. Adam Smith

3. The _____ is a measure of statistical dispersion developed by the Italian statistician Corrado Gini and published in his 1912 paper 'Variability and Mutability' (Italian: >Variabilit>à e mutabilit>à.) It is commonly used as a measure of inequality of income or wealth. It has, however, also found application in the study of inequalities in disciplines as diverse as health, ecology, and chemistry.

   a. 28-hour day
   b. Gini coefficient
   c. 33 Strategies of War
   d. 1990 Clean Air Act

4. _____ has been described as the 'process of social influence in which one person can enlist the aid and support of others in the accomplishment of a common task'. A definition more inclusive of followers comes from Alan Keith of Genentech who said '_____ is ultimately about creating a way for people to contribute to making something extraordinary happen.'

_____ is one of the most salient aspects of the organizational context. However, defining _____ has been challenging.

a. 1990 Clean Air Act
b. 28-hour day
c. Situational leadership
d. Leadership

5. _____ is a way of expressing knowledge or belief that an event will occur or has occurred. In mathematics the concept has been given an exact meaning in _____ theory, that is used extensively in such areas of study as mathematics, statistics, finance, gambling, science, and philosophy to draw conclusions about the likelihood of potential events and the underlying mechanics of complex systems.

The word _____ does not have a consistent direct definition.

a. Statistics
b. Time series analysis
c. Standard deviation
d. Probability

6. _____ in its classic form is defined as a company from one country making a physical investment into building a factory in another country. It is the establishment of an enterprise by a foreigner. Its definition can be extended to include investments made to acquire lasting interest in enterprises operating outside of the economy of the investor.
a. Compensation methods
b. Business Roundtable
c. Headquarters
d. Foreign direct investment

7. The _____ (Pub.L. 93-406, 88 Stat. 829, enacted September 2, 1974) is an American federal statute that establishes minimum standards for pension plans in private industry and provides for extensive rules on the federal income tax effects of transactions associated with employee benefit plans.
a. A Stake in the Outcome
b. Employee Retirement Income Security Act of 1974
c. AAAI
d. A4e

8. _____ is the point where a person stops employment completely. A person may also semi-retire and keep some sort of _____ job, out of choice rather than necessity. This usually happens upon reaching a determined age, when physical conditions don't allow the person to work any more (by illness or accident), or even for personal choice (usually in the presence of an adequate pension or personal savings.)

a. Termination of employment
b. Retirement
c. Wrongful dismissal
d. Severance package

Chapter 3. Business Power

1. _____ was a German philosopher, political economist, historian, political theorist, sociologist, communist and revolutionary credited as the founder of communism.

Marx summarized his approach to history and politics in the opening line of the first chapter of The Communist Manifesto : 'The history of all hitherto existing society is the history of class struggles.' Marx argued that capitalism, like previous socioeconomic systems, will produce internal tensions which will lead to its destruction. Just as capitalism replaced feudalism, socialism will in its turn replace capitalism and lead to a stateless, classless society called pure communism which will emerge after a transitional period, the 'dictatorship of the proletariat', a period sometimes referred to as the 'workers state' or 'workers' democracy' .

   a. Marxism
   b. Abraham Harold Maslow
   c. Adam Smith
   d. Karl Heinrich Marx

2. In business and accounting, _____s are everything of value that is owned by a person or company. Any property or object of value that one possesses, usually considered as applicable to the payment of one's debts is considered an _____. Simplistically stated, _____s are things of value that can be readily converted into cash.
   a. A Stake in the Outcome
   b. AAAI
   c. Asset
   d. A4e

3. In statistics, _____ is:

   - the arithmetic _____
   - the expected value of a random variable, which is also called the population _____.

It is sometimes stated that the '_____' _____s average. This is incorrect if '_____' is taken in the specific sense of 'arithmetic _____' as there are different types of averages: the _____, median, and mode. Other simple statistical analyses use measures of spread, such as range, interquartile range, or standard deviation. For a real-valued random variable X, the _____ is the expectation of X. Note that not every probability distribution has a defined _____; see the Cauchy distribution for an example.

   a. Statistical inference
   b. Control chart
   c. Correlation
   d. Mean

4. The _____ was a financial crisis that occurred in the United States when the New York Stock Exchange fell close to 50% from its peak the previous year. Panic occurred, as this was during a time of economic recession, and there were numerous runs on banks and trust companies. The 1907 panic eventually spread throughout the nation when many state and local banks and businesses entered into bankruptcy.
   a. 28-hour day
   b. 33 Strategies of War
   c. 1990 Clean Air Act
   d. Panic of 1907

5. The _____ requires the Federal government to investigate and pursue trusts, companies and organizations suspected of violating the Act. It was the first United States Federal statute to limit cartels and monopolies, and today still forms the basis for most antitrust litigation by the federal government.
   a. 1990 Clean Air Act
   b. 33 Strategies of War
   c. 28-hour day
   d. Sherman Antitrust Act

6. _____ is a form of corporate self-regulation integrated into a business model. Ideally, _____ policy would function as a built-in, self-regulating mechanism whereby business would monitor and ensure their adherence to law, ethical standards, and international norms. Business would embrace responsibility for the impact of their activities on the environment, consumers, employees, communities, stakeholders and all other members of the public sphere.
   a. 28-hour day
   b. Corporate social responsibility
   c. 1990 Clean Air Act
   d. 33 Strategies of War

Chapter 4. Critics of Business

1. _____ is an economic concept with commonplace familiarity. It is the price that a good or service is offered at, or will fetch, in the marketplace. It is of interest mainly in the study of microeconomics.
    a. 28-hour day
    b. 1990 Clean Air Act
    c. 33 Strategies of War
    d. Market price

2. _____ was a Scottish moral philosopher and a pioneer of political economy. One of the key figures of the Scottish Enlightenment, Smith is the author of The Theory of Moral Sentiments and An Inquiry into the Nature and Causes of the Wealth of Nations. The latter, usually abbreviated as The Wealth of Nations, is considered his magnum opus and the first modern work of economics.
    a. Adam Smith
    b. Affiliation
    c. Abraham Harold Maslow
    d. Affirmative action

3. The _____ was a regulatory body in the United States created by the Interstate Commerce Act of 1887, which was signed into law by President Grover Cleveland. The agency was abolished in 1995, and the agency's remaining functions were transferred to the Surface Transportation Board.

    The Commission's five members were appointed by the President with the consent of the United States Senate.

    a. Extended Enterprise
    b. United States Department of Agriculture
    c. American Institute of Industrial Engineers
    d. Interstate Commerce Commission

4. _____ is an economic and social system in which trade and industry are privately controlled for profit. The means of production, which is otherwise known as capital and includes land are owned, operated, and traded for the purpose of generating profits, without force or fraud, by private individuals either singly or jointly. Investments, distribution, income, production, pricing and supply of goods, commodities and services are determined by voluntary private decision in _____, which is also known as a market economy.
    a. Adam Smith
    b. Affiliation
    c. Abraham Harold Maslow
    d. Capitalism

5. _____ was a German philosopher, political economist, historian, political theorist, sociologist, communist and revolutionary credited as the founder of communism.

Chapter 4. Critics of Business

Marx summarized his approach to history and politics in the opening line of the first chapter of The Communist Manifesto : 'The history of all hitherto existing society is the history of class struggles.' Marx argued that capitalism, like previous socioeconomic systems, will produce internal tensions which will lead to its destruction. Just as capitalism replaced feudalism, socialism will in its turn replace capitalism and lead to a stateless, classless society called pure communism which will emerge after a transitional period, the 'dictatorship of the proletariat', a period sometimes referred to as the 'workers state' or 'workers' democracy' .

  a. Karl Heinrich Marx
  b. Adam Smith
  c. Marxism
  d. Abraham Harold Maslow

6. _____ is a term coined by Deborah E. Meyerson used to describe corporate professionals who work toward positive change in both their work environment and the way their companies conduct business -- often taking 'radical' action that is just short of getting them fired.

In her book, _____: How Everyday Leaders Inspire Change at Work (Harvard Business School Press), Meyerson describes employees who believe and work toward creating adaptive, family-friendly, and socially responsible workplaces.

_____ are quiet leaders that act as catalysts for new ideas, alternative perspectives, and organizational learning and change -- and balance company conformity with individual rebellion.

  a. Tempered Radicals
  b. 33 Strategies of War
  c. 1990 Clean Air Act
  d. 28-hour day

7. _____ is a form of corporate self-regulation integrated into a business model. Ideally, _____ policy would function as a built-in, self-regulating mechanism whereby business would monitor and ensure their adherence to law, ethical standards, and international norms. Business would embrace responsibility for the impact of their activities on the environment, consumers, employees, communities, stakeholders and all other members of the public sphere.
  a. 33 Strategies of War
  b. 28-hour day
  c. 1990 Clean Air Act
  d. Corporate social responsibility

Chapter 4. Critics of Business

8. The _____ captures an expanded spectrum of values and criteria for measuring organizational success: economic, ecological and social. With the ratification of the United Nations and ICLEI _____ standard for urban and community accounting in early 2007, this became the dominant approach to public sector full cost accounting. Similar UN standards apply to natural capital and human capital measurement to assist in measurements required by _____, e.g. the ecoBudget standard for reporting ecological footprint.
   a. Triple bottom line
   b. 28-hour day
   c. 33 Strategies of War
   d. 1990 Clean Air Act

9. A mutual _____ or stockholder is an individual or company (including a corporation) that legally owns one or more shares of stock in a joint stock company. A company's _____s collectively own that company. Thus, the typical goal of such companies is to enhance _____ value.
   a. 1990 Clean Air Act
   b. Stockholder
   c. Shareholder
   d. Free riding

10. A _____ is one scenario provided for evaluation by respondents in a Choice Experiment. Responses are collected and used to create a Choice Model. Respondents are usually provided with a series of differing _____s for evaluation.
    a. Pairwise comparison
    b. Choice Set
    c. Computerized classification test
    d. Thurstone scale

11. _____ is a concept in ethics with several meanings. It is often used synonymously with such concepts as responsibility, answerability, enforcement, blameworthiness, liability and other terms associated with the expectation of account-giving. As an aspect of governance, it has been central to discussions related to problems in both the public and private (corporation) worlds.
    a. Usury
    b. A4e
    c. A Stake in the Outcome
    d. Accountability

12. _____ is a broad philosophy and social movement regarding concerns for environmental conservation and improvement of the environment. _____ and environmental concerns may be represented with the color green.

Chapter 4. Critics of Business

_____ can also be defined as a social movement that seeks to influence the political process by lobbying, activism, and education in order to protect natural resources and ecosystems.

a. A4e
b. Industrial ecology
c. Environmentalism
d. A Stake in the Outcome

13. A _____ is an alliance among individuals or groups, during which they cooperate in joint action, each in his own self-interest, joining forces together for a common cause. This alliance may be temporary or a matter of convenience. A _____ thus differs from a more formal covenant.

a. 33 Strategies of War
b. Coalition
c. 28-hour day
d. 1990 Clean Air Act

14. _____ is the current President of Barnard College, a liberal arts college for women affiliated with Columbia University; as President of Barnard, she is also an academic dean within the university. Spar became Barnard's 11th president in 2008 after a teaching career at Harvard Business School where she was Senior Associate Dean for Faculty Research and Development. After graduating magna cum laude from the Georgetown University School of Foreign Service and earning her doctorate from Harvard in government, she went on to write 6 books and many articles.

a. John Jacob Astor
b. Bruce Edward Babbitt
c. Debora L. Spar
d. Carol Ann Bartz

15. A _____ is a name or trademark connected with a product or producer. _____s have become increasingly important components of culture and the economy, now being described as 'cultural accessories and personal philosophies'. Some people distinguish the psychological aspect of a _____ from the experiential aspect.

a. Brand extension
b. Brand awareness
c. Brand loyalty
d. Brand

Chapter 4. Critics of Business

16. The _____ is an organization that conducts food safety, public affairs, education, research, and industry relations programs for food retailers and wholesalers. _____'s membership consists of approximately 1,500 companies in 50 countries, ranging from large multi-chain stores to independent supermarkets. In the U.S., _____ members operate some 26,000 retail food stores and 14,000 pharmacies and account for about three quarters of all domestic retail food sales.
    a. Food Marketing Institute
    b. National Association of Corporate Directors
    c. National Whistleblower Center
    d. Limited liability partnership

17. _____ is an integrated communications-based process through which individuals and communities discover that existing and newly-identified needs and wants may be satisfied by the products and services of others.

    _____ is defined by the American _____ Association as the activity, set of institutions, and processes for creating, communicating, delivering, and exchanging offerings that have value for customers, clients, partners, and society at large. The term developed from the original meaning which referred literally to going to market, as in shopping, or going to a market to buy or sell goods or services.

    a. Disruptive technology
    b. Customer relationship management
    c. Marketing
    d. Market development

Chapter 5. Corporate Social Responsibility

1. _____ is a form of corporate self-regulation integrated into a business model. Ideally, _____ policy would function as a built-in, self-regulating mechanism whereby business would monitor and ensure their adherence to law, ethical standards, and international norms. Business would embrace responsibility for the impact of their activities on the environment, consumers, employees, communities, stakeholders and all other members of the public sphere.
   a. 33 Strategies of War
   b. 28-hour day
   c. 1990 Clean Air Act
   d. Corporate social responsibility

2. _____ is an economic and social system in which trade and industry are privately controlled for profit. The means of production, which is otherwise known as capital and includes land are owned, operated, and traded for the purpose of generating profits, without force or fraud, by private individuals either singly or jointly. Investments, distribution, income, production, pricing and supply of goods, commodities and services are determined by voluntary private decision in _____, which is also known as a market economy.
   a. Abraham Harold Maslow
   b. Capitalism
   c. Affiliation
   d. Adam Smith

3. _____ was a Scottish moral philosopher and a pioneer of political economy. One of the key figures of the Scottish Enlightenment, Smith is the author of The Theory of Moral Sentiments and An Inquiry into the Nature and Causes of the Wealth of Nations. The latter, usually abbreviated as The Wealth of Nations, is considered his magnum opus and the first modern work of economics.
   a. Adam Smith
   b. Affirmative action
   c. Abraham Harold Maslow
   d. Affiliation

4. _____ is a legal term that refers to a holder of property on behalf of a beneficiary. A trust can be set up either to benefit particular persons, or for any charitable purposes (but not generally for non-charitable purposes): typical examples are a will trust for the testator's children and family, a pension trust (to confer benefits on employees and their families), and a charitable trust. In all cases, the _____ may be a person or company, whether or not they are a prospective beneficiary.
   a. Hierarchical organization
   b. Commercial management
   c. Trustee
   d. Design management

Chapter 5. Corporate Social Responsibility

5. _____ is a Latin phrase that literally means 'beyond the powers'. Its inverse is called intra vires, meaning 'within the powers'. It is used as a legal term in a number of common law contexts.

In corporate law, _____ describes acts attempted by a corporation that are beyond the scope of powers granted by the corporation's Articles of Incorporation or in a clause in its Bylaws; in the laws authorizing its formation, or similar founding documents.

   a. A4e
   b. AAAI
   c. A Stake in the Outcome
   d. Ultra vires

6. The _____ is a politically conservative group of chief executive officers of major U.S. corporations formed to promote pro-business public policy.

The group was formed in 1972 through the merger of three existing organizations: the March Group, consisting of chief executive officers who met informally to consider public policy issues; the Construction Users Anti-Inflation Roundtable, a group devoted to containing construction costs; and the Labor Law Study Committee, largely made up of labor relations executives of major companies.

It 'strongly supported passage of the' No Child Left Behind Act of 2002, 'and is now actively working with states on implementation.' It has issued press releases, submitted editorials, given congressional testimony and distributed position ads.

   a. Business Roundtable
   b. National Association for the Advancement of Colored People
   c. Process-based management
   d. Headquarters

7. The _____ is an independent, non-profit, non-partisan think tank based in Washington, DC. Its membership consists of some 200 senior corporate executives and university leaders. According to its mission statement, the organization is 'dedicated to policy research on the major economic and social issues of our time and the implementation of its recommendations by the public and private sectors.'

CED's goal is to advance sound public policies that promote long-term and broad-based economic growth and opportunity for all Americans.

a. National Whistleblower Center
b. Committee for Economic Development
c. Foreign direct investment
d. Command center

8. In economics, an externality or spillover of an economic transaction is an impact on a party that is not directly involved in the transaction. In such a case, prices do not reflect the full costs or benefits in production or consumption of a product or service. A positive impact is called an external benefit, while a negative impact is called an _____.
   a. AAAI
   b. A Stake in the Outcome
   c. A4e
   d. External cost

9. In economics, business, retail, and accounting, a _____ is the value of money that has been used up to produce something, and hence is not available for use anymore. In economics, a _____ is an alternative that is given up as a result of a decision. In business, the _____ may be one of acquisition, in which case the amount of money expended to acquire it is counted as _____.
   a. Fixed costs
   b. Cost overrun
   c. Cost allocation
   d. Cost

10. _____ is a pattern of resource use that aims to meet human needs while preserving the environment so that these needs can be met not only in the present, but also for future generations. The term was used by the Brundtland Commission which coined what has become the most often-quoted definition of _____ as development that 'meets the needs of the present without compromising the ability of future generations to meet their own needs.'

_____ ties together concern for the carrying capacity of natural systems with the social challenges facing humanity. As early as the 1970s 'sustainability' was employed to describe an economy 'in equilibrium with basic ecological support systems.' Ecologists have pointed to the 'limits of growth' and presented the alternative of a 'steady state economy' in order to address environmental concerns.

   a. Sustainability reporting
   b. Sustainable business
   c. Global Reporting Initiative
   d. Sustainable Development

Chapter 5. Corporate Social Responsibility

11. The United Nations _____ is an United Nations initiative to encourage businesses worldwide to adopt sustainable and socially responsible policies, and to report on their implementation. The _____ is a principle based framework for businesses, stating ten principles in the areas of human rights, labour, the environment and anti-corruption. Under the _____, companies are brought together with UN agencies, labour groups and civil society.
    a. 33 Strategies of War
    b. Global Compact
    c. 28-hour day
    d. 1990 Clean Air Act

12. The _____ are the names of two corporate codes of conduct, developed by the African-American preacher Rev. Leon Sullivan, promoting corporate social responsibility:

    - The original _____ were developed in 1977 to apply economic pressure on South Africa in protest of its system of apartheid. The principles eventually gained wide adoption among United States-based corporations.
    - The new Global _____ were jointed unveiled in 1999 by Rev. Sullivan and United Nations Secretary General Kofi Annan. The new and expanded corporate code of conduct, as opposed to the originals' specific focus on South African apartheid, were designed to increase the active participation of corporations in the advancement of human rights and social justice at the international level.

    a. 1990 Clean Air Act
    b. Sullivan Principles
    c. 33 Strategies of War
    d. 28-hour day

13. The _____ are a set of environmental and social benchmarks for managing environmental and social issues in development project finance globally. Once adopted by banks and other financial institutions, the _____ commit the adoptees to refrain from financing projects that fail to follow the processes defined by the Principles. The _____ were developed by private sector banks - led by Citigroup, ABN AMRO, Barclays and WestLB - and were launched in June 2003.
    a. AAAI
    b. Equator Principles
    c. A Stake in the Outcome
    d. A4e

14. The _____, widely known as ISO , is an international-standard-setting body composed of representatives from various national standards organizations. Founded on 23 February 1947, the organization promulgates worldwide proprietary industrial and commercial standards. It is headquartered in Geneva, Switzerland.

a. International Organization for Standardization
b. AAAI
c. A4e
d. A Stake in the Outcome

15. A _____ is an alliance among individuals or groups, during which they cooperate in joint action, each in his own self-interest, joining forces together for a common cause. This alliance may be temporary or a matter of convenience. A _____ thus differs from a more formal covenant.
   a. 1990 Clean Air Act
   b. Coalition
   c. 28-hour day
   d. 33 Strategies of War

Chapter 6. Implementing Social Responsibility

1. _____ refers to the movement of cash into or out of a business or financial product. It is usually measured during a specified, finite period of time. Measurement of _____ can be used

   - to determine a project's rate of return or value. The time of _____s into and out of projects are used as inputs in financial models such as internal rate of return, and net present value.
   - to determine problems with a business's liquidity. Being profitable does not necessarily mean being liquid. A company can fail because of a shortage of cash, even while profitable.
   - as an alternate measure of a business's profits when it is believed that accrual accounting concepts do not represent economic realities. For example, a company may be notionally profitable but generating little operational cash (as may be the case for a company that barters its products rather than selling for cash.) In such a case, the company may be deriving additional operating cash by issuing shares evaluating default risk, re-investment requirements, etc.

   _____ is a generic term used differently depending on the context. It may be defined by users for their own purposes.

   a. Sweat equity
   b. Cash flow
   c. Gross profit
   d. Gross profit margin

2. _____ has been described as the 'process of social influence in which one person can enlist the aid and support of others in the accomplishment of a common task'. A definition more inclusive of followers comes from Alan Keith of Genentech who said '_____ is ultimately about creating a way for people to contribute to making something extraordinary happen.'

   _____ is one of the most salient aspects of the organizational context. However, defining _____ has been challenging.

   a. Leadership
   b. Situational leadership
   c. 28-hour day
   d. 1990 Clean Air Act

3. _____ is a form of corporate self-regulation integrated into a business model. Ideally, _____ policy would function as a built-in, self-regulating mechanism whereby business would monitor and ensure their adherence to law, ethical standards, and international norms. Business would embrace responsibility for the impact of their activities on the environment, consumers, employees, communities, stakeholders and all other members of the public sphere.
   a. 33 Strategies of War
   b. 1990 Clean Air Act
   c. 28-hour day
   d. Corporate social responsibility

Chapter 6. Implementing Social Responsibility

4. In business and accounting, _____s are everything of value that is owned by a person or company. Any property or object of value that one possesses, usually considered as applicable to the payment of one's debts is considered an _____. Simplistically stated, _____s are things of value that can be readily converted into cash.

   a. AAAI
   b. Asset
   c. A Stake in the Outcome
   d. A4e

5. A _____ is a framework for creating economic, social, and/or other forms of value. The term _____ is thus used for a broad range of informal and formal descriptions to represent core aspects of a business, including purpose, offerings, strategies, infrastructure, organizational structures, trading practices, and operational processes and policies.

   Conceptualizations of _____s try to formalize informal descriptions into building blocks and their relationships.

   a. Business model design
   b. Business networking
   c. Business model
   d. Gap analysis

6. A _____ is a brief written statement of the purpose of a company or organization. Ideally, a _____ guides the actions of the organization, spells out its overall goal, provides a sense of direction, and guides decision making for all levels of management.

   _____s often contain the following:

   - Purpose and aim of the organization
   - The organization's primary stakeholders: clients, stockholders, etc.
   - Responsibilities of the organization toward these stakeholders
   - Products and services offered

   In developing a _____:

   - Encourage as much input as feasible from employees, volunteers, and other stakeholders
   - Publicize it broadly

   The _____ can be used to resolve differences between business stakeholders. Stakeholders include: employees including managers and executives, stockholders, board of directors, customers, suppliers, distributors, creditors, governments (local, state, federal, etc.), unions, competitors, NGO's, and the general public.

20 Chapter 6. Implementing Social Responsibility

a. 33 Strategies of War
b. 1990 Clean Air Act
c. Mission statement
d. 28-hour day

7. The general definition of an _____ is an evaluation of a person, organization, system, process, project or product. _____s are performed to ascertain the validity and reliability of information; also to provide an assessment of a system's internal control. The goal of an _____ is to express an opinion on the person / organization/system (etc) in question, under evaluation based on work done on a test basis.

a. A Stake in the Outcome
b. Internal control
c. Audit committee
d. Audit

8. Procter is a surname, and may also refer to:

- Bryan Waller Procter (pseud. Barry Cornwall), English poet
- Goodwin Procter, American law firm
- _____, consumer products multinational

a. Strict liability
b. Downstream
c. Master and Servant Acts
d. Procter ' Gamble

9. The _____ captures an expanded spectrum of values and criteria for measuring organizational success: economic, ecological and social. With the ratification of the United Nations and ICLEI _____ standard for urban and community accounting in early 2007, this became the dominant approach to public sector full cost accounting. Similar UN standards apply to natural capital and human capital measurement to assist in measurements required by _____, e.g. the ecoBudget standard for reporting ecological footprint.

a. 33 Strategies of War
b. 28-hour day
c. 1990 Clean Air Act
d. Triple bottom line

10. The _____, 49 Stat. 1014 (Aug. 30, 1935), raised United States taxes on higher income levels, corporations, and gifts and estates.

Chapter 6. Implementing Social Responsibility

a. 1990 Clean Air Act
b. 33 Strategies of War
c. 28-hour day
d. Revenue Act of 1935

11. _____ is the deliberate pursuit of the interests or welfare of others or the public interest.

The concept has a long history in philosophical and ethical thought, and has more recently become a topic for psychologists, sociologists, evolutionary biologists, and ethologists. While ideas about _____ from one field can have an impact on the other fields, the different methods and focuses of these fields lead to different perspectives on _____.

a. A Stake in the Outcome
b. A4e
c. Altruism
d. Utilitarianism

12. _____ or cause-related marketing refers to a type of marketing involving the cooperative efforts of a 'for profit' business and a non-profit organization for mutual benefit. The term is sometimes used more broadly and generally to refer to any type of marketing effort for social and other charitable causes, including in-house marketing efforts by non-profit organizations. _____ differs from corporate giving (philanthropy) as the latter generally involves a specific donation that is tax deductible, while _____ is a marketing relationship generally not based on a donation.

a. 28-hour day
b. Cause marketing
c. 1990 Clean Air Act
d. Relationship marketing

13. _____ is an integrated communications-based process through which individuals and communities discover that existing and newly-identified needs and wants may be satisfied by the products and services of others.

_____ is defined by the American _____ Association as the activity, set of institutions, and processes for creating, communicating, delivering, and exchanging offerings that have value for customers, clients, partners, and society at large. The term developed from the original meaning which referred literally to going to market, as in shopping, or going to a market to buy or sell goods or services.

a. Marketing
b. Customer relationship management
c. Market development
d. Disruptive technology

14. The American Federation of Labor and Congress of Industrial Organizations, commonly _____, is a national trade union center, the largest federation of unions in the United States, made up of 65 national and international unions (including Canadian), together representing more than 10 million workers. It was formed in 1955 when the AFL and the CIO merged after a long estrangement. From 1955 until 2005, the _____'s member unions represented nearly all unionized workers in the United States.
    a. AFL-CIO
    b. United Mine Workers
    c. A4e
    d. A Stake in the Outcome

Chapter 7. Business Ethics

1. _____ is a form of applied ethics that examines ethical principles and moral or ethical problems that arise in a business environment. It applies to all aspects of business conduct and is relevant to the conduct of individuals and business organizations as a whole. Applied ethics is a field of ethics that deals with ethical questions in many fields such as medical, technical, legal and _____.
   a. Hypernorms
   b. Corporate Sustainability
   c. Facilitation payments
   d. Business ethics

2. The U.S. _____ is an independent agency of the United States government which holds primary responsibility for enforcing the federal securities laws and regulating the securities industry, the nation's stock and options exchanges, and other electronic securities markets. The SEC was created by section 4 of the Securities Exchange Act of 1934 (now codified as 15 U.S.C. § 78d and commonly referred to as the 1934 Act.)
   a. 1990 Clean Air Act
   b. 28-hour day
   c. 33 Strategies of War
   d. Securities and Exchange Commission

3. _____ was a Scottish moral philosopher and a pioneer of political economy. One of the key figures of the Scottish Enlightenment, Smith is the author of The Theory of Moral Sentiments and An Inquiry into the Nature and Causes of the Wealth of Nations. The latter, usually abbreviated as The Wealth of Nations, is considered his magnum opus and the first modern work of economics.
   a. Affiliation
   b. Affirmative action
   c. Abraham Harold Maslow
   d. Adam Smith

4. In philosophy _____ is the position that moral or ethical propositions do not reflect objective and/or universal moral truths, but instead make claims relative to social, cultural, historical or personal circumstances. Moral relativists hold that no universal standard exists by which to assess an ethical proposition's truth. Relativistic positions often see moral values as applicable only within certain cultural boundaries (cultural relativism) or in the context of individual preferences (individualist ethical subjectivism.)
   a. 1990 Clean Air Act
   b. 28-hour day
   c. Moral absolutism
   d. Moral relativism

5. _____ are a concept from Business ethics that applies to principles so fundamental that, by definition, they serve to evaluate lower-order norms, reaching to the root of what is ethical for humanity.

They were first proposed Thomas Donaldson and Thomas W. Dunfee as part of an integrative social contract model of business ethics. Donaldson and Dunfee have described _____ as:

'principles so fundamental that they constitute norms by which all others are to be judged.'

a. Sexual harassment
b. 28-hour day
c. 1990 Clean Air Act
d. Hypernorms

6. _____ are paid to compensate the claimant for loss, injury, or harm suffered by another's breach of duty.

On a breach of contract by a defendant, a court generally awards the sum which would restore the injured party to the economic position that he or she expected from performance of the promise or promises.

When it is either not possible or desirable to award damages measured in that way, a court may award money damages designed to restore the injured party to the economic position that he or she had occupied at the time the contract was entered, or designed to prevent the breaching party from being unjustly enriched

a. 33 Strategies of War
b. 28-hour day
c. 1990 Clean Air Act
d. Compensatory damages

7. The _____ is the primary federal law in the United States governing water pollution. The act established the symbolic goals of eliminating releases to water of high amounts of toxic substances, eliminating additional water pollution by 1985, and ensuring that surface waters would meet standards necessary for human sports and recreation by 1983.

The principal body of law currently in effect is based on the Federal Water Pollution Control Amendments of 1972, which significantly expanded and strengthened earlier legislation.

a. Regulatory compliance
b. Non-disclosure agreement
c. Foreign Corrupt Practices Act
d. Clean Water Act

Chapter 7. Business Ethics

8. The _____ of 2002 (Pub.L. 107-204, 116 Stat. 745, enacted July 30, 2002), also known as the Public Company Accounting Reform and Investor Protection Act of 2002 and commonly called Sarbanes-Oxley, Sarbox or SOX, is a United States federal law enacted on July 30, 2002, as a reaction to a number of major corporate and accounting scandals including those affecting Enron, Tyco International, Adelphia, Peregrine Systems and WorldCom.
   a. Sarbanes-Oxley Act of 2002
   b. Sarbanes-Oxley Act
   c. Fair Labor Standards Act
   d. Letter of credit

9. A _____ is a relatively new executive level position at a corporation, company, organization typically reporting directly to the CEO or board of directors. The _____ is responsible for a brand's image, experience, and promise, and propagating it throughout all aspects of the company. The brand officer oversees marketing, advertising, design, public relations and customer service departments.
   a. Director of communications
   b. Purchasing manager
   c. Chief executive officer
   d. Chief brand officer

10. _____ has been described as the 'process of social influence in which one person can enlist the aid and support of others in the accomplishment of a common task'. A definition more inclusive of followers comes from Alan Keith of Genentech who said '_____ is ultimately about creating a way for people to contribute to making something extraordinary happen.'

    _____ is one of the most salient aspects of the organizational context. However, defining _____ has been challenging.

    a. 1990 Clean Air Act
    b. Leadership
    c. 28-hour day
    d. Situational leadership

11. Organizational culture is not the same as _____. It is wider and deeper concepts, something that an organization 'is' rather than what it 'has' (according to Buchanan and Huczynski.)

    _____ is the total sum of the values, customs, traditions and meanings that make a company unique.

a. Corporate culture
b. Work design
c. Job analysis
d. Path-goal theory

12. A _____ is a set of rules outlining the responsibilities of or proper practices for an individual or organization. Related concepts include ethical codes and honor codes.

In its 2007 International Good Practice Guidance, Defining and Developing an Effective _____ for Organizations, the International Federation of Accountants provided the following working definition:

'Principles, values, standards, or rules of behavior that guide the decisions, procedures and systems of an organization in a way that (a) contributes to the welfare of its key stakeholders, and (b) respects the rights of all constituents affected by its operations.'

a. 33 Strategies of War
b. Code of conduct
c. 1990 Clean Air Act
d. 28-hour day

Chapter 8. Making Ethical Decisions in Business 27

1. _____ is an advertisement in which a particular product specifically mentions a competitor by name for the express purpose of showing why the competitor is inferior to the product naming it.

This should not be confused with parody advertisements, where a fictional product is being advertised for the purpose of poking fun at the particular advertisement, nor should it be confused with the use of a coined brand name for the purpose of comparing the product without actually naming an actual competitor. ('Wikipedia tastes better and is less filling than the Encyclopedia Galactica.')

In the 1980s, during what has been referred to as the cola wars, soft-drink manufacturer Pepsi ran a series of advertisements where people, caught on hidden camera, in a blind taste test, chose Pepsi over rival Coca-Cola.

   a. 28-hour day
   b. 1990 Clean Air Act
   c. 33 Strategies of War
   d. Comparative advertising

2. In statistics, _____ is:

   - the arithmetic _____
   - the expected value of a random variable, which is also called the population _____.

It is sometimes stated that the '_____' _____s average. This is incorrect if '_____' is taken in the specific sense of 'arithmetic _____' as there are different types of averages: the _____, median, and mode. Other simple statistical analyses use measures of spread, such as range, interquartile range, or standard deviation. For a real-valued random variable X, the _____ is the expectation of X. Note that not every probability distribution has a defined _____; see the Cauchy distribution for an example.

   a. Control chart
   b. Correlation
   c. Statistical inference
   d. Mean

3. The U.S. _____ is an independent agency of the United States government which holds primary responsibility for enforcing the federal securities laws and regulating the securities industry, the nation's stock and options exchanges, and other electronic securities markets. The SEC was created by section 4 of the Securities Exchange Act of 1934 (now codified as 15 U.S.C. § 78d and commonly referred to as the 1934 Act.)
   a. 28-hour day
   b. 1990 Clean Air Act
   c. 33 Strategies of War
   d. Securities and Exchange Commission

Chapter 8. Making Ethical Decisions in Business

4. _____ is a cross-disciplinary area concerned with protecting the safety, health and welfare of people engaged in work or employment. The goal of all _____ programs is to foster a work free safe environment. As a secondary effect, it may also protect co-workers, family members, employers, customers, suppliers, nearby communities, and other members of the public who are impacted by the workplace environment.
   a. AAAI
   b. Occupational Safety and Health
   c. A Stake in the Outcome
   d. A4e

5. The _____ is the primary federal law which governs occupational health and safety in the private sector and federal government in the United States. It was enacted by Congress in 1970 and was signed by President Richard Nixon on December 29, 1970. Its main goal is to ensure that employers provide employees with an environment free from recognized hazards, such as exposure to toxic chemicals, excessive noise levels, mechanical dangers, heat or cold stress, or unsanitary conditions.
   a. Unemployment Action Center
   b. Unemployment and Farm Relief Act
   c. United States Department of Justice
   d. Occupational Safety and Health Act

6. The _____ is an American federal law which allows people who are not affiliated with the government to file actions against federal contractors claiming fraud against the government. The act of filing such actions is informally called 'whistleblowing.' Persons filing under the Act stand to receive a portion (usually about 15-25 percent) of any recovered damages.
   a. Chrapliwy v. Uniroyal
   b. False Claims Act
   c. Personal Responsibility and Work Opportunity Reconciliation Act
   d. Bennett Amendment

Chapter 9. Business in Politics

1. The _____ was the name that United States President Franklin D. Roosevelt gave to a complex package of economic programs he initiated between 1933 and 1935 with the goal of giving relief to the unemployed, reform of business and financial practices, and promoting recovery of the economy during The Great Depression.

When Franklin Delano Roosevelt took office on March 4, 1933, the nation was deeply troubled. Banks in 37 states were closed and many checks could not be cashed.

   a. 28-hour day
   b. New Deal
   c. 1990 Clean Air Act
   d. 33 Strategies of War

2. _____ is a broad label that refers to any individuals or households that use goods and services generated within the economy. The concept of a _____ is used in different contexts, so that the usage and significance of the term may vary.

Typically when business people and economists talk of _____s they are talking about person as _____, an aggregated commodity item with little individuality other than that expressed in the buy/not-buy decision.

   a. 28-hour day
   b. 33 Strategies of War
   c. Consumer
   d. 1990 Clean Air Act

3. The _____ is a politically conservative group of chief executive officers of major U.S. corporations formed to promote pro-business public policy.

The group was formed in 1972 through the merger of three existing organizations: the March Group, consisting of chief executive officers who met informally to consider public policy issues; the Construction Users Anti-Inflation Roundtable, a group devoted to containing construction costs; and the Labor Law Study Committee, largely made up of labor relations executives of major companies.

It 'strongly supported passage of the' No Child Left Behind Act of 2002, 'and is now actively working with states on implementation.' It has issued press releases, submitted editorials, given congressional testimony and distributed position ads.

Chapter 9. Business in Politics

   a. Business Roundtable
   b. Process-based management
   c. Headquarters
   d. National Association for the Advancement of Colored People

4. An _____ is an organization founded and funded by businesses that operate in a specific industry. An industry trade association participates in public relations activities such as advertising, education, political donations, lobbying and publishing, but its main focus is collaboration between companies, or standardization. Associations may offer other services, such as producing conferences, networking or charitable events or offering classes or educational materials.
   a. AAAI
   b. A Stake in the Outcome
   c. Industry trade group
   d. A4e

5. A _____ is an alliance among individuals or groups, during which they cooperate in joint action, each in his own self-interest, joining forces together for a common cause. This alliance may be temporary or a matter of convenience. A _____ thus differs from a more formal covenant.
   a. 28-hour day
   b. 1990 Clean Air Act
   c. 33 Strategies of War
   d. Coalition

6. _____ is a form of communication that typically attempts to persuade potential customers to purchase or to consume more of a particular brand of product or service. 'While now central to the contemporary global economy and the reproduction of global production networks, it is only quite recently that _____ has been more than a marginal influence on patterns of sales and production. The formation of modern _____ was intimately bound up with the emergence of new forms of monopoly capitalism around the end of the 19th and beginning of the 20th century as one element in corporate strategies to create, organize and where possible control markets, especially for mass produced consumer goods.
   a. A4e
   b. A Stake in the Outcome
   c. AAAI
   d. Advertising

7. _____ is an advertisement in which a particular product specifically mentions a competitor by name for the express purpose of showing why the competitor is inferior to the product naming it.

Chapter 9. Business in Politics

This should not be confused with parody advertisements, where a fictional product is being advertised for the purpose of poking fun at the particular advertisement, nor should it be confused with the use of a coined brand name for the purpose of comparing the product without actually naming an actual competitor. ('Wikipedia tastes better and is less filling than the Encyclopedia Galactica.')

In the 1980s, during what has been referred to as the cola wars, soft-drink manufacturer Pepsi ran a series of advertisements where people, caught on hidden camera, in a blind taste test, chose Pepsi over rival Coca-Cola.

   a. 33 Strategies of War
   b. 1990 Clean Air Act
   c. Comparative advertising
   d. 28-hour day

8. A _____ is a company that owns other companies' outstanding stock. It usually refers to a company which does not produce goods or services itself, rather its only purpose is owning shares of other companies. Holding companies allow the reduction of risk for the owners and can allow the ownership and control of a number of different companies.
   a. Holding Company
   b. Prometric
   c. National Association for the Advancement of Colored People
   d. Multinational corporation

9. The _____ of 1935 was a law that was passed by the United States Congress to facilitate regulation of electric utilities, by either limiting their operations to a single state, and thus subjecting them to effective state regulation, or forcing divestitures so that each became a single integrated system serving a limited geographic area. Another purpose of _____ was to keep utility holding companies engaged in regulated businesses from engaging in unregulated businesses. _____ required that Securities and Exchange Commission (SEC) approval be obtained by a holding company prior to engaging in a non-utility business and that such businesses be kept separate from the regulated business(es.)
   a. 28-hour day
   b. Pure Food and Drug Act
   c. 1990 Clean Air Act
   d. Public Utility Holding Company Act

10. The U.S. _____ is an independent agency of the United States government which holds primary responsibility for enforcing the federal securities laws and regulating the securities industry, the nation's stock and options exchanges, and other electronic securities markets. The SEC was created by section 4 of the Securities Exchange Act of 1934 (now codified as 15 U.S.C. Â§ 78d and commonly referred to as the 1934 Act.)

a. 28-hour day
b. 33 Strategies of War
c. 1990 Clean Air Act
d. Securities and Exchange Commission

11. In economics, _____ is a measure of the relative satisfaction from consumption of various goods and services. Given this measure, one may speak meaningfully of increasing or decreasing _____, and thereby explain economic behavior in terms of attempts to increase one's _____. For illustrative purposes, changes in _____ are sometimes expressed in units called utils.
   a. A Stake in the Outcome
   b. Ordinal utility
   c. Utility
   d. Indirect utility function

Chapter 10. Federal Regulation of Business

1. _____ is a contract between two parties, one being the employer and the other being the employee. An employee may be defined as: 'A person in the service of another under any contract of hire, express or implied, oral or written, where the employer has the power or right to control and direct the employee in the material details of how the work is to be performed.' Black's Law Dictionary page 471 (5th ed. 1979.)
    a. Exit interview
    b. Employment
    c. Employment counsellor
    d. Employment rate

2. The term _____ was created by President Lyndon B. Johnson when he signed Executive Order 11246 on September 24, 1965, created to prohibit federal contractors from discriminating against employees on the basis of race, sex, creed, religion, color, or national origin. In more recent times, most employers have also added sexual orientation to the list of non-discrimination.

    The Executive Order also required contractors to implement affirmative action plans to increase the participation of minorities and women in the workplace.

    a. A4e
    b. A Stake in the Outcome
    c. AAAI
    d. Equal Employment Opportunity

3. The U.S. _____ is a federal agency whose goal is ending employment discrimination. The _____ investigates discrimination complaints based on an individual's race, color, national origin, religion, sex, age, disability and retaliation for reporting and/or opposing a discriminatory practice. The Commission is also tasked with filing suits on behalf of alleged victim(s) of discrimination against employers and as an adjudicatory for claims of discrimination brought against federal agencies.
    a. Airbus SAS
    b. ARCO
    c. Equal Employment Opportunity Commission
    d. Airbus Industrie

4. Many negative _____ are related to the environmental consequences of production and use

    - Systemic risk describes the risks to the overall economy arising from the risks which the banking system takes. That the private costs of banking failure may be smaller than the social costs justifies banking regulations, although regulations could create a moral hazard.

    - Anthropogenic climate change is attributed to greenhouse gas emissions from burning oil, gas, and coal. Global warming has been ranked as the #1 externality of all economic activity, in the magnitude of potential harms and yet remains unmitigated.

a. A Stake in the Outcome
b. AAAI
c. A4e
d. Externalities

5. In economics, a _____ occurs when, due to the economies of scale of a particular industry, the maximum efficiency of production and distribution is realized through a single supplier.

A _____ arises where the largest supplier in an industry, often the first supplier in a market, has an overwhelming cost advantage over other actual or potential competitors. This tends to be the case in industries where capital costs predominate, creating economies of scale which are large in relation to the size of the market, and hence high barriers to entry; examples include water services and electricity.

a. Free rider problem
b. 1990 Clean Air Act
c. 28-hour day
d. Natural monopoly

6. In economics, a _____ exists when a specific individual or enterprise has sufficient control over a particular product or service to determine significantly the terms on which other individuals shall have access to it. Monopolies are thus characterized by a lack of economic competition for the good or service that they provide and a lack of viable substitute goods. The verb 'monopolize' refers to the process by which a firm gains persistently greater market share than what is expected under perfect competition.

a. 1990 Clean Air Act
b. 33 Strategies of War
c. 28-hour day
d. Monopoly

7. _____ is an advertisement in which a particular product specifically mentions a competitor by name for the express purpose of showing why the competitor is inferior to the product naming it.

This should not be confused with parody advertisements, where a fictional product is being advertised for the purpose of poking fun at the particular advertisement, nor should it be confused with the use of a coined brand name for the purpose of comparing the product without actually naming an actual competitor. ('Wikipedia tastes better and is less filling than the Encyclopedia Galactica.')

In the 1980s, during what has been referred to as the cola wars, soft-drink manufacturer Pepsi ran a series of advertisements where people, caught on hidden camera, in a blind taste test, chose Pepsi over rival Coca-Cola.

a. Comparative advertising
b. 33 Strategies of War
c. 1990 Clean Air Act
d. 28-hour day

8. The _____ was the name that United States President Franklin D. Roosevelt gave to a complex package of economic programs he initiated between 1933 and 1935 with the goal of giving relief to the unemployed, reform of business and financial practices, and promoting recovery of the economy during The Great Depression.

When Franklin Delano Roosevelt took office on March 4, 1933, the nation was deeply troubled. Banks in 37 states were closed and many checks could not be cashed.

a. 28-hour day
b. 33 Strategies of War
c. 1990 Clean Air Act
d. New Deal

9. The _____ of 1990 (ADA) is the short title of United States (Pub.L. 101-336, 104 Stat. 327, enacted July 26, 1990), codified at 42 U.S.C. § 12101 et seq. It was signed into law on July 26, 1990, by President George H. W. Bush, and later amended with changes effective January 1, 2009. The ADA is a wide-ranging civil rights law that prohibits, under certain circumstances, discrimination based on disability. It affords similar protections against discrimination to Americans with disabilities as the Civil Rights Act of 1964,
a. Australian labour law
b. Equal Pay Act of 1963
c. Americans with Disabilities Act
d. Employment discrimination

10. _____ generally refers to a list of all planned expenses and revenues. It is a plan for saving and spending. A _____ is an important concept in microeconomics, which uses a _____ line to illustrate the trade-offs between two or more goods.
a. 1990 Clean Air Act
b. Budget
c. 33 Strategies of War
d. 28-hour day

11. The _____ is an enumerated power listed in the United States Constitution (Article 1, Section 8, Clause 3). The clause states that Congress has the power to regulate commerce with foreign nations, among the states, and with the Native American tribes. Courts and commentators have tended to discuss each of these three areas of commerce as a separate power granted to the Congress of the United States.
   a. 1990 Clean Air Act
   b. 28-hour day
   c. 33 Strategies of War
   d. Commerce clause

12. _____, 17 U.S. (4 Wheat.) 518 (1819), was a landmark United States Supreme Court case dealing with the application of the Contract Clause of the United States Constitution to private corporations. The case arose when the president of Dartmouth College was deposed by its trustees, leading to the New Hampshire legislature attempting to force the College to become a public institution and thereby place the ability to appoint trustees in the hands of the governor.
   a. Civil Rights Act of 1991
   b. Bennett Amendment
   c. Regulatory compliance
   d. Trustees of Dartmouth College v. Woodward

13. The _____ was a regulatory body in the United States created by the Interstate Commerce Act of 1887, which was signed into law by President Grover Cleveland. The agency was abolished in 1995, and the agency's remaining functions were transferred to the Surface Transportation Board.

The Commission's five members were appointed by the President with the consent of the United States Senate.

   a. Extended Enterprise
   b. United States Department of Agriculture
   c. American Institute of Industrial Engineers
   d. Interstate Commerce Commission

14. The _____ of 1906 was a United States federal law that authorized the Secretary of Agriculture to inspect and condemn any meat product found unfit for human consumption. Unlike previous laws ordering meat inspections which were enforced to assure European nations from banning pork trade, this law was strongly motivated to protect the American diet. All labels on any type of food had to be accurate (although not all ingredients were provided on the label.)
   a. Contrat nouvelle embauche
   b. Federal Trade Commission Act
   c. Civil Rights Act of 1991
   d. Meat Inspection Act

Chapter 10. Federal Regulation of Business

15. _____, 94 U.S. 113 (1876), was a United States Supreme Court case dealing with corporate rates and agriculture. The Munn case allowed states to regulate certain businesses within their borders, including railroads, and is commonly regarded as a milestone in the growth of federal government regulation.

This case involved the famous opinion delivered by Chief Justice Morrison Remick Waite (1816-1888.)

 a. Munn v. Illinois
 b. Covenant
 c. Ricci v. DeStefano
 d. Privacy Act of 1974

16. The _____ requires the Federal government to investigate and pursue trusts, companies and organizations suspected of violating the Act. It was the first United States Federal statute to limit cartels and monopolies, and today still forms the basis for most antitrust litigation by the federal government.
 a. Sherman Antitrust Act
 b. 33 Strategies of War
 c. 28-hour day
 d. 1990 Clean Air Act

17. The field of _____ looks at the relationship between management and workers, particularly groups of workers represented by a union.

_____ is an important factor in analyzing 'varieties of capitalism', such as neocorporatism, social democracy, and neoliberalism

 a. Organizational effectiveness
 b. Informal organization
 c. Overtime
 d. Industrial relations

18. The _____ is a 1935 United States federal law that limits the means with which employers may react to workers in the private sector that organize labor unions, engage in collective bargaining, and take part in strikes and other forms of concerted activity in support of their demands. The Act does not, on the other hand, cover those workers who are covered by the Railway Labor Act, agricultural employees, domestic employees, supervisors, independent contractors and some close relatives of individual employers.

It was in a context of severe economic troubles that the Wagner Act came into effect.

Chapter 10. Federal Regulation of Business

a. National Labor Relations Act
b. 33 Strategies of War
c. 1990 Clean Air Act
d. 28-hour day

19. A _____ is a relatively new executive level position at a corporation, company, organization typically reporting directly to the CEO or board of directors. The _____ is responsible for a brand's image, experience, and promise, and propagating it throughout all aspects of the company. The brand officer oversees marketing, advertising, design, public relations and customer service departments.
   a. Director of communications
   b. Chief executive officer
   c. Purchasing manager
   d. Chief brand officer

20. In economics, business, retail, and accounting, a _____ is the value of money that has been used up to produce something, and hence is not available for use anymore. In economics, a _____ is an alternative that is given up as a result of a decision. In business, the _____ may be one of acquisition, in which case the amount of money expended to acquire it is counted as _____.
   a. Cost overrun
   b. Cost allocation
   c. Fixed costs
   d. Cost

21. In economics, _____ is the desire to own something and the ability to pay for it. The term _____ signifies the ability or the willingness to buy a particular commodity at a given point of time.
   a. Demand
   b. 33 Strategies of War
   c. 1990 Clean Air Act
   d. 28-hour day

22. The _____ of June 30, 1906 is a United States federal law that provided federal inspection of meat products and forbade the manufacture, sale, or transportation of adulterated food products and poisonous patent medicines. The Act arose due to public education and expos>és from Muckrakers such as Upton Sinclair and Samuel Hopkins Adams, social activist Florence Kelley, researcher Harvey W. Wiley, and President Theodore Roosevelt.

The _____ was initially concerned with ensuring products were labeled correctly.

a. Public Utility Holding Company Act
b. 28-hour day
c. 1990 Clean Air Act
d. Pure Food and Drug Act

23. The United States Federal _____ to oversee the safety of food, drugs, and cosmetics. A principal author of this law was Royal S. Copeland, a three-term U.S. Senator from New York. In 1968, the Electronic Product Radiation Control provisions were added to the FD'C.

a. Partnership
b. Comprehensive Environmental Response, Compensation, and Liability Act
c. Rulemaking
d. Food, Drug, and Cosmetic Act

24. Procter is a surname, and may also refer to:

- Bryan Waller Procter (pseud. Barry Cornwall), English poet
- Goodwin Procter, American law firm
- _____, consumer products multinational

a. Strict liability
b. Master and Servant Acts
c. Downstream
d. Procter ' Gamble

Chapter 11. Reforming Regulation

1. _____ is a broad label that refers to any individuals or households that use goods and services generated within the economy. The concept of a _____ is used in different contexts, so that the usage and significance of the term may vary.

Typically when business people and economists talk of _____s they are talking about person as _____, an aggregated commodity item with little individuality other than that expressed in the buy/not-buy decision.

   a. 28-hour day
   b. 1990 Clean Air Act
   c. 33 Strategies of War
   d. Consumer

2. _____ is a cross-disciplinary area concerned with protecting the safety, health and welfare of people engaged in work or employment. The goal of all _____ programs is to foster a work free safe environment. As a secondary effect, it may also protect co-workers, family members, employers, customers, suppliers, nearby communities, and other members of the public who are impacted by the workplace environment.
   a. AAAI
   b. A Stake in the Outcome
   c. A4e
   d. Occupational Safety and Health

3. The _____ is the primary federal law which governs occupational health and safety in the private sector and federal government in the United States. It was enacted by Congress in 1970 and was signed by President Richard Nixon on December 29, 1970. Its main goal is to ensure that employers provide employees with an environment free from recognized hazards, such as exposure to toxic chemicals, excessive noise levels, mechanical dangers, heat or cold stress, or unsanitary conditions.
   a. Unemployment and Farm Relief Act
   b. Unemployment Action Center
   c. United States Department of Justice
   d. Occupational Safety and Health Act

4. _____ generally refers to a list of all planned expenses and revenues. It is a plan for saving and spending. A _____ is an important concept in microeconomics, which uses a _____ line to illustrate the trade-offs between two or more goods.
   a. 33 Strategies of War
   b. 28-hour day
   c. 1990 Clean Air Act
   d. Budget

Chapter 11. Reforming Regulation

5. _____ is the incidence or process of transferring ownership of a business, enterprise, agency or public service from the public sector (government) to the private sector (business.) In a broader sense, _____ refers to transfer of any government function to the private sector including governmental functions like revenue collection and law enforcement.
   a. Performance reports
   b. 1990 Clean Air Act
   c. Privatization
   d. 28-hour day

6. The U.S. _____ is an independent agency of the United States government which holds primary responsibility for enforcing the federal securities laws and regulating the securities industry, the nation's stock and options exchanges, and other electronic securities markets. The SEC was created by section 4 of the Securities Exchange Act of 1934 (now codified as 15 U.S.C. Â§ 78d and commonly referred to as the 1934 Act.)
   a. 28-hour day
   b. 33 Strategies of War
   c. 1990 Clean Air Act
   d. Securities and Exchange Commission

7. _____ is the removal or simplification of government rules and regulations that constrain the operation of market forces. _____ does not mean elimination of laws against fraud, but eliminating or reducing government control of how business is done, thereby moving toward a more free market.

   The stated rationale for '_____' is often that fewer and simpler regulations will lead to a raised level of competitiveness, therefore higher productivity, more efficiency and lower prices overall.

   a. Natural rate of unemployment
   b. Value added
   c. Deregulation
   d. Rehn-Meidner Model

8. The _____ is a United States federal law signed into law on October 24, 1978. The main purpose of the act was to remove government control over fares, routes and market entry (of new airlines) from commercial aviation.
   a. A Stake in the Outcome
   b. Airline Deregulation Act
   c. A4e
   d. AAAI

Chapter 11. Reforming Regulation

9. A _____ is a relatively new executive level position at a corporation, company, organization typically reporting directly to the CEO or board of directors. The _____ is responsible for a brand's image, experience, and promise, and propagating it throughout all aspects of the company. The brand officer oversees marketing, advertising, design, public relations and customer service departments.
    a. Director of communications
    b. Chief executive officer
    c. Chief brand officer
    d. Purchasing manager

10. In economics and sociology, an _____ is any factor (financial or non-financial) that enables or motivates a particular course of action, or counts as a reason for preferring one choice to the alternatives. It is an expectation that encourages people to behave in a certain way. Since human beings are purposeful creatures, the study of _____ structures is central to the study of all economic activity (both in terms of individual decision-making and in terms of co-operation and competition within a larger institutional structure.)
    a. A Stake in the Outcome
    b. Incentive
    c. AAAI
    d. A4e

11. _____ is one of the managerial functions like planning, organizing, staffing and directing. It is an important function because it helps to check the errors and to take the corrective action so that deviation from standards are minimized and stated goals of the organization are achieved in desired manner. According to modern concepts, _____ is a foreseeing action whereas earlier concept of _____ was used only when errors were detected. _____ in management means setting standards, measuring actual performance and taking corrective action.
    a. Decision tree pruning
    b. Schedule of reinforcement
    c. Turnover
    d. Control

Chapter 11. Reforming Regulation

12. _____, known in the United States as antitrust law, has three main elements:

   - prohibiting agreements or practices that restrict free trading and competition between business entities. This includes in particular the repression of cartels.
   - banning abusive behavior by a firm dominating a market, or anti-competitive practices that tend to lead to such a dominant position. Practices controlled in this way may include predatory pricing, tying, price gouging, refusal to deal, and many others.
   - supervising the mergers and acquisitions of large corporations, including some joint ventures. Transactions that are considered to threaten the competitive process can be prohibited altogether, or approved subject to 'remedies' such as an obligation to divest part of the merged business or to offer licenses or access to facilities to enable other businesses to continue competing.

The substance and practice of _____ varies from jurisdiction to jurisdiction. Protecting the interests of consumers (consumer welfare) and ensuring that entrepreneurs have an opportunity to compete in the market economy are often treated as important objectives. _____ is closely connected with law on deregulation of access to markets, state aids and subsidies, the privatization of state owned assets and the establishment of independent sector regulators. In recent decades, _____ has been viewed as a way to provide better public services.

   a. Competition law
   b. Federal Employers Liability Act
   c. Rulemaking
   d. Right to Financial Privacy Act

13. The _____ is an independent agency of the United States government, established in 1914 by the _____ Act. Its principal mission is the promotion of 'consumer protection' and the elimination and prevention of what regulators perceive to be harmfully 'anti-competitive' business practices, such as coercive monopoly.

The _____ Act was one of President Wilson's major acts against trusts.

   a. 1990 Clean Air Act
   b. 28-hour day
   c. 33 Strategies of War
   d. Federal Trade Commission

14. The _____ of 1914 (15 U.S.C §§ 41-58, as amended) established the Federal Trade Commission (FTC), a bipartisan body of five members appointed by the President of the United States for seven year terms. This Commission was authorized to issue Cease and Desist orders to large corporations to curb unfair trade practices. This Act also gave more flexibility to the US congress for judicial matters.

a. Resource Conservation and Recovery Act
b. Sarbanes-Oxley Act of 2002
c. Comprehensive Environmental Response, Compensation, and Liability Act
d. Federal Trade Commission Act

15. _____ exists when sales of identical goods or services are transacted at different prices from the same provider. In a theoretical market with perfect information, no transaction costs or prohibition on secondary exchange (or re-selling) to prevent arbitrage, _____ can only be a feature of monopoly and oligopoly markets, where market power can be exercised. Otherwise, the moment the seller tries to sell the same good at different prices, the buyer at the lower price can arbitrage by selling to the consumer buying at the higher price but with a tiny discount.
    a. Price points
    b. Target costing
    c. Pricing objectives
    d. Price discrimination

16. The _____ requires the Federal government to investigate and pursue trusts, companies and organizations suspected of violating the Act. It was the first United States Federal statute to limit cartels and monopolies, and today still forms the basis for most antitrust litigation by the federal government.
    a. 28-hour day
    b. 33 Strategies of War
    c. 1990 Clean Air Act
    d. Sherman Antitrust Act

17. The _____ of 1938 is a United States federal law that amended the Federal Trade Commission Act to add the clause 'unfair or deceptive acts or practices in commerce are hereby declared unlawful' to the Section 5 prohibition of unfair methods of competition, in order to protect consumers as well as competition.

1938 amendment to the federal trade commission act that authorized the FTC to restrict unfair or deceptive acts; also called the advertising act. Until this amendment was passed, the FTC could only restrict practices that were unfair to competitors.

   a. Reverification
   b. Financial Security Law of France
   c. Wheeler-Lea Act
   d. Drug test

Chapter 11. Reforming Regulation

18. A _____ is officially defined as being 'any merger that is not horizontal or vertical; in general, it is the combination of firms in different industries or firms operating in different geographic areas'. _____s can serve various purposes, including extending corporate territories and extending a product range. One example of a _____ was the merger between the Walt Disney Company and the American Broadcasting Company.

   a. Private placement
   b. Choquet integral
   c. Conglomerate merger
   d. Manufacturing operations

19. In economics, a _____ is the combination of two or more firms competing in the same market with the same good or service. See Horizontal integration.

   a. 33 Strategies of War
   b. 28-hour day
   c. 1990 Clean Air Act
   d. Horizontal merger

20. The term '_____' refers to the concept of collecting information and attempting to spot a pattern in the information. In some fields of study, the term '_____' has more formally-defined meanings.

   In project management _____ is a mathematical technique that uses historical results to predict future outcome.

   a. Regression analysis
   b. Stepwise regression
   c. Least squares
   d. Trend analysis

Chapter 12. Multinational Corporations and Trade

1. _____ in its literal sense is the process of transformation of local or regional phenomena into global ones. It can be described as a process by which the people of the world are unified into a single society and function together.

This process is a combination of economic, technological, sociocultural and political forces.

   a. Collaborative Planning, Forecasting and Replenishment
   b. Cost Management
   c. Globalization
   d. Histogram

2. _____ in its classic form is defined as a company from one country making a physical investment into building a factory in another country. It is the establishment of an enterprise by a foreigner. Its definition can be extended to include investments made to acquire lasting interest in enterprises operating outside of the economy of the investor.
   a. Foreign direct investment
   b. Business Roundtable
   c. Headquarters
   d. Compensation methods

3. A _____ or transnational corporation is a corporation or enterprise that manages production or delivers services in more than one country. It can also be referred to as an international corporation.

The first modern _____ is generally thought to be the Dutch East India Company, established in 1602.

   a. Financial Accounting Standards Board
   b. Small and medium enterprises
   c. Multinational corporation
   d. Command center

4. A _____ is a country that has low standards of democratic governments, civil service, industrialization, social programs, and/or human rights guarantees that are yet to 'develop' to those met in the West or alternative goals of material progress (not necessarily a clone of those of the West.) It is often a term used to describe a nation with a low level of material well being. Despite this definition, the levels of development may vary, with some developing countries having higher average standards of living.
   a. 28-hour day
   b. Developing country
   c. 1990 Clean Air Act
   d. 33 Strategies of War

Chapter 12. Multinational Corporations and Trade

5. _____ is a type of trade policy that allows traders to act and transact without interference from government. Thus, the policy permits trading partners mutual gains from trade, with goods and services produced according to the theory of comparative advantage.

Under a _____ policy, prices are a reflection of true supply and demand, and are the sole determinant of resource allocation.

a. 28-hour day
b. 1990 Clean Air Act
c. 33 Strategies of War
d. Free trade

6. In economics, _____ refers to the ability of a person or a country to produce a particular good at a lower marginal cost and opportunity cost than another person or country. It is the ability to produce a product most efficiently given all the other products that could be produced. It can be contrasted with absolute advantage which refers to the ability of a person or a country to produce a particular good at a lower absolute cost than another.

a. 28-hour day
b. 33 Strategies of War
c. 1990 Clean Air Act
d. Comparative advantage

7. _____ is a designated group of countries that have agreed to eliminate tariffs, quotas and preferences on most (if not all) goods and services traded between them. It can be considered the second stage of economic integration. Countries choose this kind of economic integration form if their economical structures are complementary.

a. 1990 Clean Air Act
b. 28-hour day
c. 33 Strategies of War
d. Free trade area

8. The _____ was the outcome of the failure of negotiating governments to create the International Trade Organization (ITO.) GATT was formed in 1947 and lasted until 1994, when it was replaced by the World Trade Organization. The Bretton Woods Conference had introduced the idea for an organization to regulate trade as part of a larger plan for economic recovery after World War II.

a. 1990 Clean Air Act
b. 28-hour day
c. General Agreement on Tariffs and Trade
d. Multilateral treaty

Chapter 12. Multinational Corporations and Trade

9. The _____ is a trilateral trade bloc in North America created by the governments of the United States, Canada, and Mexico. The agreement creating the trade bloc came into force on January 1, 1994. It superseded the Canada-United States Free Trade Agreement between the U.S. and Canada.

   a. Career portfolios
   b. North American Free Trade Agreement
   c. Business war game
   d. Trade union

10. _____ is an advertisement in which a particular product specifically mentions a competitor by name for the express purpose of showing why the competitor is inferior to the product naming it.

This should not be confused with parody advertisements, where a fictional product is being advertised for the purpose of poking fun at the particular advertisement, nor should it be confused with the use of a coined brand name for the purpose of comparing the product without actually naming an actual competitor. ('Wikipedia tastes better and is less filling than the Encyclopedia Galactica.')

In the 1980s, during what has been referred to as the cola wars, soft-drink manufacturer Pepsi ran a series of advertisements where people, caught on hidden camera, in a blind taste test, chose Pepsi over rival Coca-Cola.

   a. 33 Strategies of War
   b. 28-hour day
   c. Comparative advertising
   d. 1990 Clean Air Act

11. _____ is, in very basic words, a position a firm occupies against its competitors.

According to Michael Porter, the three methods for creating a sustainable _____ are through:

1. Cost leadership

2. Differentiation

3. Focus (economics)

   a. 28-hour day
   b. Competitive advantage
   c. Theory Z
   d. 1990 Clean Air Act

Chapter 12. Multinational Corporations and Trade

12. The _____ of 1977 (15 U.S.C. §§ 78dd-1, et seq.) is a United States federal law known primarily for two of its main provisions, one that addresses accounting transparency requirements under the Securities Exchange Act of 1934 and another concerning bribery of foreign officials.

   a. Social Security Act of 1965
   b. Meritor Savings Bank v. Vinson
   c. Foreign Corrupt Practices Act
   d. Limited liability

13. The U.S. _____ is an independent agency of the United States government which holds primary responsibility for enforcing the federal securities laws and regulating the securities industry, the nation's stock and options exchanges, and other electronic securities markets. The SEC was created by section 4 of the Securities Exchange Act of 1934 (now codified as 15 U.S.C. § 78d and commonly referred to as the 1934 Act.)

   a. 33 Strategies of War
   b. 1990 Clean Air Act
   c. Securities and Exchange Commission
   d. 28-hour day

14. The _____ or Bhopal gas tragedy was an industrial disaster that took place at a Union Carbide pesticide plant in the Indian city of Bhopal, Madhya Pradesh. On 3 December 1984, the plant released 42 tonnes of toxic methyl isocyanate (MIC) gas, exposing more than 500,000 people to toxic gases. The first official immediate death toll was 2,259.

   a. Bhopal disaster
   b. 28-hour day
   c. 1990 Clean Air Act
   d. 33 Strategies of War

Chapter 13. Globalization

1. _____ in its literal sense is the process of transformation of local or regional phenomena into global ones. It can be described as a process by which the people of the world are unified into a single society and function together.

This process is a combination of economic, technological, sociocultural and political forces.

   a. Histogram
   b. Globalization
   c. Cost Management
   d. Collaborative Planning, Forecasting and Replenishment

2. _____ is Distinguished University Professor at the University of Maryland, College Park. A largely self-taught sociologist, Ritzer is most widely known in the scholarly community for his distinctive contributions to the study of consumption, globalization, metatheory, and modern and postmodern social theory generally. Ritzer is an academic celebrity, however, as a result of The McDonaldization of Society (4th edition 2004; first published in 1993), which is among the most popular monographs ever penned by a sociologist.
   a. Donald M. Berwick
   b. Clotaire Rapaille
   c. Brian McLean
   d. George Ritzer

3. A _____ or transnational corporation is a corporation or enterprise that manages production or delivers services in more than one country. It can also be referred to as an international corporation.

The first modern _____ is generally thought to be the Dutch East India Company, established in 1602.

   a. Small and medium enterprises
   b. Financial Accounting Standards Board
   c. Command center
   d. Multinational corporation

4. _____ is a type of trade policy that allows traders to act and transact without interference from government. Thus, the policy permits trading partners mutual gains from trade, with goods and services produced according to the theory of comparative advantage.

Under a _____ policy, prices are a reflection of true supply and demand, and are the sole determinant of resource allocation.

a. 1990 Clean Air Act
b. 33 Strategies of War
c. Free Trade
d. 28-hour day

5. _____ is a designated group of countries that have agreed to eliminate tariffs, quotas and preferences on most (if not all) goods and services traded between them. It can be considered the second stage of economic integration. Countries choose this kind of economic integration form if their economical structures are complementary.
   a. 28-hour day
   b. 1990 Clean Air Act
   c. 33 Strategies of War
   d. Free trade area

6. The _____ is a trilateral trade bloc in North America created by the governments of the United States, Canada, and Mexico. The agreement creating the trade bloc came into force on January 1, 1994. It superseded the Canada-United States Free Trade Agreement between the U.S. and Canada.
   a. Business war game
   b. North American Free Trade Agreement
   c. Career portfolios
   d. Trade union

7. A _____ or maquila is a factory that imports materials and equipment on a duty-free and tariff-free basis for assembly or manufacturing and then re-exports the assembled product, usually back to the originating country. A maquila is also referred to as a 'twin plant', or 'in-bond' industry. Nearly half a million Mexicans are employed in _____s.
   a. 28-hour day
   b. 33 Strategies of War
   c. 1990 Clean Air Act
   d. Maquiladora

8. _____ is an economic and social system in which trade and industry are privately controlled for profit. The means of production, which is otherwise known as capital and includes land are owned, operated, and traded for the purpose of generating profits, without force or fraud, by private individuals either singly or jointly. Investments, distribution, income, production, pricing and supply of goods, commodities and services are determined by voluntary private decision in _____, which is also known as a market economy.

a. Adam Smith
b. Capitalism
c. Affiliation
d. Abraham Harold Maslow

9. _____ is a pejorative term describing an allegedly capitalist economy in which success in business depends on close relationships between businesspeople and government officials. It may be exhibited by favoritism in the distribution of legal permits, government grants, special tax breaks, and so forth.

_____ is believed to arise when political cronyism spills over into the business world; self-serving friendships and family ties between businessmen and the government influence the economy and society to the extent that it corrupts public-serving economic and political ideals.

a. 28-hour day
b. Global Corruption Report
c. Crony capitalism
d. 1990 Clean Air Act

10. _____ was a writer, management consultant, and self-described 'social ecologist.' Widely considered to be 'the father of modern management,' his 39 books and countless scholarly and popular articles explored how humans are organized across all sectors of society--in business, government and the nonprofit world. His writings have predicted many of the major developments of the late twentieth century, including privatization and decentralization; the rise of Japan to economic world power; the decisive importance of marketing; and the emergence of the information society with its necessity of lifelong learning. In 1959, Drucker coined the term 'knowledge worker' and later in his life considered knowledge work productivity to be the next frontier of management.
a. Jacques Al-Salawat Nasruddin Nasser
b. Debora L. Spar
c. Peter Ferdinand Drucker
d. Chrissie Hynde

11. The _____ was the outcome of the failure of negotiating governments to create the International Trade Organization (ITO.) GATT was formed in 1947 and lasted until 1994, when it was replaced by the World Trade Organization. The Bretton Woods Conference had introduced the idea for an organization to regulate trade as part of a larger plan for economic recovery after World War II.
a. 28-hour day
b. 1990 Clean Air Act
c. General Agreement on Tariffs and Trade
d. Multilateral treaty

12. A _____ is a country that has low standards of democratic governments, civil service, industrialization, social programs, and/or human rights guarantees that are yet to 'develop' to those met in the West or alternative goals of material progress (not necessarily a clone of those of the West.) It is often a term used to describe a nation with a low level of material well being. Despite this definition, the levels of development may vary, with some developing countries having higher average standards of living.
   a. 33 Strategies of War
   b. Developing country
   c. 28-hour day
   d. 1990 Clean Air Act

Chapter 14. Industrial Pollution and Environmental Policy

1. _____ is an advertisement in which a particular product specifically mentions a competitor by name for the express purpose of showing why the competitor is inferior to the product naming it.

This should not be confused with parody advertisements, where a fictional product is being advertised for the purpose of poking fun at the particular advertisement, nor should it be confused with the use of a coined brand name for the purpose of comparing the product without actually naming an actual competitor. ('Wikipedia tastes better and is less filling than the Encyclopedia Galactica.')

In the 1980s, during what has been referred to as the cola wars, soft-drink manufacturer Pepsi ran a series of advertisements where people, caught on hidden camera, in a blind taste test, chose Pepsi over rival Coca-Cola.

a. 33 Strategies of War
b. 1990 Clean Air Act
c. 28-hour day
d. Comparative advertising

2. A _____ is typically described as a deliberate plan of action to guide decisions and achieve rational outcome(s.) However, the term may also be used to denote what is actually done, even though it is unplanned.

The term may apply to government, private sector organizations and groups, and individuals.

a. 33 Strategies of War
b. Policy
c. 1990 Clean Air Act
d. 28-hour day

3. _____ is a pattern of resource use that aims to meet human needs while preserving the environment so that these needs can be met not only in the present, but also for future generations. The term was used by the Brundtland Commission which coined what has become the most often-quoted definition of _____ as development that 'meets the needs of the present without compromising the ability of future generations to meet their own needs.'

_____ ties together concern for the carrying capacity of natural systems with the social challenges facing humanity. As early as the 1970s 'sustainability' was employed to describe an economy 'in equilibrium with basic ecological support systems.' Ecologists have pointed to the 'limits of growth' and presented the alternative of a 'steady state economy' in order to address environmental concerns.

a. Sustainable development
b. Sustainability reporting
c. Global Reporting Initiative
d. Sustainable business

Chapter 14. Industrial Pollution and Environmental Policy

4. _____ is an economic and social system in which trade and industry are privately controlled for profit. The means of production, which is otherwise known as capital and includes land are owned, operated, and traded for the purpose of generating profits, without force or fraud, by private individuals either singly or jointly. Investments, distribution, income, production, pricing and supply of goods, commodities and services are determined by voluntary private decision in _____, which is also known as a market economy.
    a. Adam Smith
    b. Affiliation
    c. Abraham Harold Maslow
    d. Capitalism

5. _____ was a Scottish moral philosopher and a pioneer of political economy. One of the key figures of the Scottish Enlightenment, Smith is the author of The Theory of Moral Sentiments and An Inquiry into the Nature and Causes of the Wealth of Nations. The latter, usually abbreviated as The Wealth of Nations, is considered his magnum opus and the first modern work of economics.
    a. Adam Smith
    b. Affirmative action
    c. Abraham Harold Maslow
    d. Affiliation

6. _____ is one of the managerial functions like planning, organizing, staffing and directing. It is an important function because it helps to check the errors and to take the corrective action so that deviation from standards are minimized and stated goals of the organization are achieved in desired manner. According to modern concepts, _____ is a foreseeing action whereas earlier concept of _____ was used only when errors were detected. _____ in management means setting standards, measuring actual performance and taking corrective action.
    a. Schedule of reinforcement
    b. Decision tree pruning
    c. Turnover
    d. Control

7. _____ generally refers to a list of all planned expenses and revenues. It is a plan for saving and spending. A _____ is an important concept in microeconomics, which uses a _____ line to illustrate the trade-offs between two or more goods.
    a. 28-hour day
    b. Budget
    c. 33 Strategies of War
    d. 1990 Clean Air Act

Chapter 14. Industrial Pollution and Environmental Policy

8. The _____ is the primary federal law in the United States governing water pollution. The act established the symbolic goals of eliminating releases to water of high amounts of toxic substances, eliminating additional water pollution by 1985, and ensuring that surface waters would meet standards necessary for human sports and recreation by 1983.

The principal body of law currently in effect is based on the Federal Water Pollution Control Amendments of 1972, which significantly expanded and strengthened earlier legislation.

   a. Foreign Corrupt Practices Act
   b. Non-disclosure agreement
   c. Regulatory compliance
   d. Clean Water Act

9. An _____ can be defined as the average emission rate of a given pollutant for a given source, relative to the intensity of a specific activity. _____s are used to derive estimates of air pollutant or greenhouse gas emissions based on the amount of fuel combusted, the number of animals in animal husbandry, on industrial production levels, distances traveled or similar activity data.

_____s assume a linear relation between the intensity of the activity and the emission resulting from this activity:

$Emission_{pollutant}$ = Activity * _____$_{pollutant}$

The level of uncertainty of the resulting estimates depends significantly on the source category and the pollutant.

   a. A4e
   b. A Stake in the Outcome
   c. Exhaust gas
   d. Emission factor

10. The _____, enacted in 1976, is the principal Federal law in the United States governing the disposal of solid waste and hazardous waste.

Congress enacted RCRA to address the increasing problems the nation faced from its growing volume of municipal and industrial waste. RCRA, which amended the Solid Waste Disposal Act of 1965, set national goals for:

- Protecting human health and the environment from the potential hazards of waste disposal.
- Conserving energy and natural resources.
- Reducing the amount of waste generated.
- Ensuring that wastes are managed in an environmentally-sound manner.

Chapter 14. Industrial Pollution and Environmental Policy 57

EPA waste management regulations are codified at 40 C.F.R. pts. 239-282.

a. Social Security Act of 1965
b. New Negro Alliance v. Sanitary Grocery Co.
c. Resource Conservation and Recovery Act
d. Food, Drug, and Cosmetic Act

11. The _____ is a United States law, passed by the United States Congress in 1976, that regulates the introduction of new or already existing chemicals. It grandfathered most existing chemicals, in contrast to the Registration, Evaluation and Authorization of Chemicals (REACH) legislation of the European Union. However, as explained below, the _____ specifically regulates polychlorinated biphenyl (PCB) products.

a. Federal Employers Liability Act
b. National treatment
c. Toxic Substances Control Act
d. Drug test

12. The _____ is the Cabinet department of the United States government concerned with promoting economic growth. It was originally created as the _____ and Labor on February 14, 1903. It was subsequently renamed to the Department of Commerce on March 4, 1913, and its bureaus and agencies specializing in labor were transferred to the new Department of Labor.

a. United States Department of Commerce
b. A Stake in the Outcome
c. AAAI
d. A4e

13. The 'business case for _____', theorizes that in a global marketplace, a company that employs a diverse workforce (both men and women, people of many generations, people from ethnically and racially diverse backgrounds etc.) is better able to understand the demographics of the marketplace it serves and is thus better equipped to thrive in that marketplace than a company that has a more limited range of employee demographics.

An additional corollary suggests that a company that supports the _____ of its workforce can also improve employee satisfaction, productivity and retention.

a. Virtual team
b. Trademark
c. Diversity
d. Kanban

Chapter 15. Managing Environmental Quality

1. A _____ is typically described as a deliberate plan of action to guide decisions and achieve rational outcome(s.) However, the term may also be used to denote what is actually done, even though it is unplanned.

   The term may apply to government, private sector organizations and groups, and individuals.

   a. 28-hour day
   b. 33 Strategies of War
   c. 1990 Clean Air Act
   d. Policy

2. In decision theory and estimation theory, the _____ of an estimator, $\hat{\theta}$, of an unknown parameter of the distribution, θ, is the expected value of the loss function

$$R(\theta, \hat{\theta}) = \mathbb{E}_\theta L(\theta, \hat{\theta}) = \int L(\theta, \hat{\theta})\, dP_\theta.$$

where dP_θ is a probability measure parametrized by θ.

- For a scalar parameter θ and a quadratic loss function,

$$L(\theta, \hat{\theta}) = (\theta - \hat{\theta})^2$$

   the _____ function becomes the mean squared error of the estimate,

$$R(\theta, \hat{\theta}) = E_\theta(\theta - \hat{\theta})^2$$

- In density estimation, the unknown parameter is probability density itself. The loss function is typically chosen to be a norm in an appropriate function space. For example, for L^2 norm,

$$L(f, \hat{f}) = \|f - \hat{f}\|_2^2$$

   the _____ function becomes the mean integrated squared error

$$R(f, \hat{f}) = E\|f - \hat{f}\|^2$$

Chapter 15. Managing Environmental Quality 59

a. Risk
b. Risk aversion
c. Financial modeling
d. Linear model

3. _____ is a step in a risk management process. _____ is the determination of quantitative or qualitative value of risk related to a concrete situation and a recognized threat (also called hazard.) Quantitative _____ requires calculations of two components of risk: R, the magnitude of the potential loss L, and the probability p, that the loss will occur.
   a. 28-hour day
   b. 1990 Clean Air Act
   c. Quality assurance
   d. Risk assessment

4. _____ is the identification, assessment, and prioritization of risks followed by coordinated and economical application of resources to minimize, monitor, and control the probability and/or impact of unfortunate events.. Risks can come from uncertainty in financial markets, project failures, legal liabilities, credit risk, accidents, natural causes and disasters as well as deliberate attacks from an adversary. Several _____ standards have been developed including the Project Management Institute, the National Institute of Science and Technology, actuarial societies, and ISO standards.
   a. Kanban
   b. Succession planning
   c. Trademark
   d. Risk management

5. _____ generally refers to a list of all planned expenses and revenues. It is a plan for saving and spending. A _____ is an important concept in microeconomics, which uses a _____ line to illustrate the trade-offs between two or more goods.
   a. 1990 Clean Air Act
   b. 28-hour day
   c. 33 Strategies of War
   d. Budget

6. _____ is a term that refers both to:

   - a formal discipline used to help appraise, or assess, the case for a project or proposal, which itself is a process known as project appraisal; and
   - an informal approach to making decisions of any kind.

Under both definitions the process involves, whether explicitly or implicitly, weighing the total expected costs against the total expected benefits of one or more actions in order to choose the best or most profitable option. The formal process is often referred to as either CBA (_____) or BCost-benefit analysis

A hallmark of CBA is that all benefits and all costs are expressed in money terms, and are adjusted for the time value of money, so that all flows of benefits and flows of project costs over time (which tend to occur at different points in time) are expressed on a common basis in terms of their 'present value.' Closely related, but slightly different, formal techniques include Cost-effectiveness analysis, Economic impact analysis, Fiscal impact analysis and Social Return on Investment(SROI) analysis. The latter builds upon the logic of _____, but differs in that it is explicitly designed to inform the practical decision-making of enterprise managers and investors focused on optimising their social and environmental impacts.

   a. Kepner-Tregoe
   b. Decision engineering
   c. Gittins index
   d. Cost-benefit analysis

7. _____ is a survey-based economic technique for the valuation of non-market resources, such as environmental preservation or the impact of contamination. While these resources do give people utility, certain aspects of them do not have a market price as they are not directly sold--for example, people receive benefit from a beautiful view of a mountain, but it would be tough to value using price-based models. _____ surveys are one technique which is used to measure these aspects.
   a. 28-hour day
   b. 33 Strategies of War
   c. 1990 Clean Air Act
   d. Contingent valuation

8. In economics and sociology, an _____ is any factor (financial or non-financial) that enables or motivates a particular course of action, or counts as a reason for preferring one choice to the alternatives. It is an expectation that encourages people to behave in a certain way. Since human beings are purposeful creatures, the study of _____ structures is central to the study of all economic activity (both in terms of individual decision-making and in terms of co-operation and competition within a larger institutional structure.)
   a. AAAI
   b. A4e
   c. A Stake in the Outcome
   d. Incentive

Chapter 15. Managing Environmental Quality

9. _____ refers to the movement of cash into or out of a business or financial product. It is usually measured during a specified, finite period of time. Measurement of _____ can be used

- to determine a project's rate of return or value. The time of _____s into and out of projects are used as inputs in financial models such as internal rate of return, and net present value.
- to determine problems with a business's liquidity. Being profitable does not necessarily mean being liquid. A company can fail because of a shortage of cash, even while profitable.
- as an alternate measure of a business's profits when it is believed that accrual accounting concepts do not represent economic realities. For example, a company may be notionally profitable but generating little operational cash (as may be the case for a company that barters its products rather than selling for cash.) In such a case, the company may be deriving additional operating cash by issuing shares evaluating default risk, re-investment requirements, etc.

_____ is a generic term used differently depending on the context. It may be defined by users for their own purposes.

a. Gross profit
b. Sweat equity
c. Cash flow
d. Gross profit margin

10. The _____, widely known as ISO , is an international-standard-setting body composed of representatives from various national standards organizations. Founded on 23 February 1947, the organization promulgates worldwide proprietary industrial and commercial standards. It is headquartered in Geneva, Switzerland.

a. A4e
b. AAAI
c. A Stake in the Outcome
d. International Organization for Standardization

11. _____ is an economic and social system in which trade and industry are privately controlled for profit. The means of production, which is otherwise known as capital and includes land are owned, operated, and traded for the purpose of generating profits, without force or fraud, by private individuals either singly or jointly. Investments, distribution, income, production, pricing and supply of goods, commodities and services are determined by voluntary private decision in _____, which is also known as a market economy.

a. Capitalism
b. Affiliation
c. Abraham Harold Maslow
d. Adam Smith

12. _____: Creating the Next Industrial Revolution is a 1999 book co-authored by Paul Hawken, Amory Lovins and Hunter Lovins. It has been translated into a dozen languages and was the subject of a Harvard Business Review summary.

In _____ the authors see the world's economy as being within the larger economy of natural resources and ecosystem services that sustain us.

a. 1990 Clean Air Act
b. 33 Strategies of War
c. 28-hour day
d. Natural capitalism

13. The _____ is a moral and political principle which states that if an action or policy might cause severe or irreversible harm to the public or to the environment, in the absence of a scientific consensus that harm would not ensue, the burden of proof falls on those who would advocate taking the action. The principle implies that there is a responsibility to intervene and protect the public from exposure to harm where scientific investigation discovers a plausible risk in the course of having screened for other suspected causes. The protections that mitigate suspected risks can be relaxed only if further scientific findings emerge that more robustly support an alternative explanation.

a. 1990 Clean Air Act
b. 28-hour day
c. Natural rights
d. Precautionary principle

14. Procter is a surname, and may also refer to:

- Bryan Waller Procter (pseud. Barry Cornwall), English poet
- Goodwin Procter, American law firm
- _____, consumer products multinational

a. Strict liability
b. Procter ' Gamble
c. Downstream
d. Master and Servant Acts

Chapter 16. Consumerism

1. _____ is the equation of personal happiness with consumption and the purchase of material possessions. The term is often associated with criticisms of consumption starting with Thorstein Veblen or, more recently by a movement called Enoughism.

Veblen's subject of examination, the newly emergent middle class arising at the turn of the twentieth century, comes to full fruition by the end of the twentieth century through the process of globalization.

In economics, _____ refers to economic policies placing emphasis on consumption.

  a. 28-hour day
  b. 1990 Clean Air Act
  c. Consumerism
  d. Market culture

2. The _____ of June 30, 1906 is a United States federal law that provided federal inspection of meat products and forbade the manufacture, sale, or transportation of adulterated food products and poisonous patent medicines. The Act arose due to public education and expos>és from Muckrakers such as Upton Sinclair and Samuel Hopkins Adams, social activist Florence Kelley, researcher Harvey W. Wiley, and President Theodore Roosevelt.

The _____ was initially concerned with ensuring products were labeled correctly.

  a. Public Utility Holding Company Act
  b. Pure Food and Drug Act
  c. 28-hour day
  d. 1990 Clean Air Act

3. _____ is a broad label that refers to any individuals or households that use goods and services generated within the economy. The concept of a _____ is used in different contexts, so that the usage and significance of the term may vary.

Typically when business people and economists talk of _____s they are talking about person as _____, an aggregated commodity item with little individuality other than that expressed in the buy/not-buy decision.

  a. 33 Strategies of War
  b. 28-hour day
  c. Consumer
  d. 1990 Clean Air Act

Chapter 16. Consumerism

4. The United States _____ is an independent agency of the United States government created in 1972 through the Consumer Product Safety Act to protect 'against unreasonable risks of injuries associated with consumer products.' As of 2006 its acting chairman is Nancy Nord, a Republican. The other commissioner is Thomas Hill Moore, a Democrat. Normally the board has three commissioners.
   a. 28-hour day
   b. Consumer Product Safety Commission
   c. 1990 Clean Air Act
   d. 33 Strategies of War

5. The _____ is an agency of the United States Department of Health and Human Services and is responsible for regulating and supervising the safety of foods, dietary supplements, drugs, vaccines, biological medical products, blood products, medical devices, radiation-emitting devices, veterinary products, and cosmetics. The FDA also enforces section 361 of the Public Health Service Act and the associated regulations, including sanitation requirements on interstate travel as well as specific rules for control of disease on products ranging from pet turtles to semen donations for assisted reproductive medicine techniques.

The FDA is an agency within the United States Department of Health and Human Services responsible for protecting and promoting the nation's public health.

   a. 33 Strategies of War
   b. 28-hour day
   c. 1990 Clean Air Act
   d. Food and Drug Administration

6. _____ is the area of law in which manufacturers, distributors, suppliers, retailers, and others who make products available to the public are held responsible for the injuries those products cause.

In the United States, the claims most commonly associated with _____ are negligence, strict liability, breach of warranty, and various consumer protection claims. The majority of _____ laws are determined at the state level and vary widely from state to state.

   a. Right-to-work laws
   b. Leave of absence
   c. Railway Labor Act
   d. Product liability

7. A _____ is a relatively new executive level position at a corporation, company, organization typically reporting directly to the CEO or board of directors. The _____ is responsible for a brand's image, experience, and promise, and propagating it throughout all aspects of the company. The brand officer oversees marketing, advertising, design, public relations and customer service departments.

Chapter 16. Consumerism

a. Chief brand officer
b. Director of communications
c. Purchasing manager
d. Chief executive officer

8. _____ laws are designed to ensure fair competition and the free flow of truthful information in the marketplace. The laws are designed to prevent businesses that engage in fraud or specified unfair practices from gaining an advantage over competitors and may provide additional protection for the weak and unable to take care of themselves. _____ laws are a form of government regulation which protects the interests of consumers.

   a. Sarbanes-Oxley Act
   b. Certificate of Incorporation
   c. Comprehensive Environmental Response, Compensation, and Liability Act
   d. Consumer Protection

9. The United States Federal _____ to oversee the safety of food, drugs, and cosmetics. A principal author of this law was Royal S. Copeland, a three-term U.S. Senator from New York. In 1968, the Electronic Product Radiation Control provisions were added to the FD'C.

   a. Partnership
   b. Comprehensive Environmental Response, Compensation, and Liability Act
   c. Rulemaking
   d. Food, Drug, and Cosmetic Act

10. _____ is a contract between two parties, one being the employer and the other being the employee. An employee may be defined as: 'A person in the service of another under any contract of hire, express or implied, oral or written, where the employer has the power or right to control and direct the employee in the material details of how the work is to be performed.' Black's Law Dictionary page 471 (5th ed. 1979.)

    a. Employment
    b. Employment counsellor
    c. Employment rate
    d. Exit interview

11. The term _____ was created by President Lyndon B. Johnson when he signed Executive Order 11246 on September 24, 1965, created to prohibit federal contractors from discriminating against employees on the basis of race, sex, creed, religion, color, or national origin. In more recent times, most employers have also added sexual orientation to the list of non-discrimination.

The Executive Order also required contractors to implement affirmative action plans to increase the participation of minorities and women in the workplace.

a. AAAI
b. A4e
c. Equal Employment Opportunity
d. A Stake in the Outcome

12. The U.S. _____ is a federal agency whose goal is ending employment discrimination. The _____ investigates discrimination complaints based on an individual's race, color, national origin, religion, sex, age, disability and retaliation for reporting and/or opposing a discriminatory practice. The Commission is also tasked with filing suits on behalf of alleged victim(s) of discrimination against employers and as an adjudicatory for claims of discrimination brought against federal agencies.

a. Equal Employment Opportunity Commission
b. Airbus Industrie
c. ARCO
d. Airbus SAS

13. The act of becoming a surety is also called a _____. Traditionally a _____ was distinguished from a surety in that the surety's liability was joint and primary with the principal, whereas the guaranty's liability was ancillary and derivative, but many jurisdictions have abolished this distinction

a. National treatment
b. Blue sky law
c. Clayton Antitrust Act
d. Guarantee

14. In general, a _____ is an arrangement to provide people with an income when they are no longer earning a regular income from employment.

The terms retirement plan or superannuation refer to a _____ granted upon retirement. Retirement plans may be set up by employers, insurance companies, the government or other institutions such as employer associations or trade unions.

a. State Compensation Insurance Fund
b. Pension insurance contract
c. Wage
d. Pension

15. The U.S. _____ is an independent agency of the United States government which holds primary responsibility for enforcing the federal securities laws and regulating the securities industry, the nation's stock and options exchanges, and other electronic securities markets. The SEC was created by section 4 of the Securities Exchange Act of 1934 (now codified as 15 U.S.C. Â§ 78d and commonly referred to as the 1934 Act.)
   a. 33 Strategies of War
   b. 1990 Clean Air Act
   c. 28-hour day
   d. Securities and Exchange Commission

16. _____ is an advertisement in which a particular product specifically mentions a competitor by name for the express purpose of showing why the competitor is inferior to the product naming it.

This should not be confused with parody advertisements, where a fictional product is being advertised for the purpose of poking fun at the particular advertisement, nor should it be confused with the use of a coined brand name for the purpose of comparing the product without actually naming an actual competitor. ('Wikipedia tastes better and is less filling than the Encyclopedia Galactica.')

In the 1980s, during what has been referred to as the cola wars, soft-drink manufacturer Pepsi ran a series of advertisements where people, caught on hidden camera, in a blind taste test, chose Pepsi over rival Coca-Cola.

   a. Comparative advertising
   b. 1990 Clean Air Act
   c. 33 Strategies of War
   d. 28-hour day

17. _____ is a legal concept in the common law legal systems usually used to achieve compensation for injuries (not accidents.) _____ is a type of tort or delict (also known as a civil wrong.)
   a. Certificate of Incorporation
   b. Mediation
   c. Diminishing returns
   d. Negligence

18. The doctrine of _____ in contract law provides that a contract cannot confer rights or impose obligations arising under it on any person or agent except the parties to it.

The premise is that only parties to contracts should be able to sue to enforce their rights or claim damages as such. However, the doctrine has proven problematic due to its implications upon contracts made for the benefit of third parties who are unable to enforce the obligations of the contracting parties.

a. Privacy Act of 1974
b. Comprehensive Environmental Response, Compensation, and Liability Act
c. Blue sky law
d. Privity

19. An _____ is quite usually a standard guarantee from the seller of a product that specifies the extent to which the quality or performance of the product is assured and states the conditions under which the product can be returned, replaced, or repaired. It is often given in the form of a specific, written 'Warranty' document. However, a warranty may also arise by operation of law based upon the seller's description of the goods, and perhaps their source and quality, and any material deviation from that specification would violate the guarantee.

a. AAAI
b. A Stake in the Outcome
c. Express warranty
d. A4e

20. In common law jurisdictions, an _____ is a contract law term for certain assurances that are presumed to be made in the sale of products or real property, due to the circumstances of the sale. These assurances are characterized as warranties irrespective of whether the seller has expressly promised them orally or in writing. They include an _____ of fitness for a particular purpose, an _____ of merchantability for products, _____ of workmanlike quality for services, and an _____ of habitability for a home.

a. A Stake in the Outcome
b. A4e
c. AAAI
d. Implied warranty

21. _____, 217 N.Y. 382, 111 N.E. 1050 (1916) is the famous New York Court of Appeals opinion by Judge Benjamin N. Cardozo which removed privity from duty in negligence actions.

The plaintiff, Donald C. MacPherson, was injured when one of the wooden wheels of his automobile crumbled. The defendant, Buick Motor Company, had manufactured the vehicle, but not the wheel, which had been manufactured by another party and installed by defendant. It was conceded that the defective wheel could have been discovered upon inspection. The defendant denied liability because the plaintiff had purchased the automobile from a dealer, not directly from the defendant.

a. MacPherson v. Buick Motor Co.
b. Letter of credit
c. Partnership agreement
d. Contrat nouvelle embauche

Chapter 16. Consumerism

22. _____ makes a person responsible for the damage and loss caused by his/her acts and omissions regardless of culpability. _____ is important in torts (especially product liability), corporations law, and criminal law.

   a. Ten year occupational employment projection
   b. Historiometry
   c. Competency-based job descriptions
   d. Strict liability

23. _____ is a form of communication that typically attempts to persuade potential customers to purchase or to consume more of a particular brand of product or service. 'While now central to the contemporary global economy and the reproduction of global production networks, it is only quite recently that _____ has been more than a marginal influence on patterns of sales and production. The formation of modern _____ was intimately bound up with the emergence of new forms of monopoly capitalism around the end of the 19th and beginning of the 20th century as one element in corporate strategies to create, organize and where possible control markets, especially for mass produced consumer goods.

   a. AAAI
   b. A Stake in the Outcome
   c. Advertising
   d. A4e

24. _____ is an integrated communications-based process through which individuals and communities discover that existing and newly-identified needs and wants may be satisfied by the products and services of others.

   _____ is defined by the American _____ Association as the activity, set of institutions, and processes for creating, communicating, delivering, and exchanging offerings that have value for customers, clients, partners, and society at large. The term developed from the original meaning which referred literally to going to market, as in shopping, or going to a market to buy or sell goods or services.

   a. Marketing
   b. Customer relationship management
   c. Market development
   d. Disruptive technology

Chapter 17. The Changing Workplace

1. The field of _____ looks at the relationship between management and workers, particularly groups of workers represented by a union.

   _____ is an important factor in analyzing 'varieties of capitalism', such as neocorporatism, social democracy, and neoliberalism

   a. Industrial relations
   b. Informal organization
   c. Organizational effectiveness
   d. Overtime

2. The _____ is a 1935 United States federal law that limits the means with which employers may react to workers in the private sector that organize labor unions, engage in collective bargaining, and take part in strikes and other forms of concerted activity in support of their demands. The Act does not, on the other hand, cover those workers who are covered by the Railway Labor Act, agricultural employees, domestic employees, supervisors, independent contractors and some close relatives of individual employers.

   It was in a context of severe economic troubles that the Wagner Act came into effect.

   a. 33 Strategies of War
   b. 28-hour day
   c. 1990 Clean Air Act
   d. National Labor Relations Act

3. _____ or _____ data refers to selected population characteristics as used in government, marketing or opinion research, or the _____ profiles used in such research. Note the distinction from the term 'demography' Commonly-used _____s include race, age, income, disabilities, mobility (in terms of travel time to work or number of vehicles available), educational attainment, home ownership, employment status, and even location.
   a. Abraham Harold Maslow
   b. Adam Smith
   c. Affiliation
   d. Demographic

4. _____ is a mathematical science pertaining to the collection, analysis, interpretation or explanation, and presentation of data. It also provides tools for prediction and forecasting based on data. It is applicable to a wide variety of academic disciplines, from the natural and social sciences to the humanities, government and business.

a. Simple moving average
b. Failure rate
c. Statistics
d. Location parameter

5. _____ is an advertisement in which a particular product specifically mentions a competitor by name for the express purpose of showing why the competitor is inferior to the product naming it.

This should not be confused with parody advertisements, where a fictional product is being advertised for the purpose of poking fun at the particular advertisement, nor should it be confused with the use of a coined brand name for the purpose of comparing the product without actually naming an actual competitor. ('Wikipedia tastes better and is less filling than the Encyclopedia Galactica.')

In the 1980s, during what has been referred to as the cola wars, soft-drink manufacturer Pepsi ran a series of advertisements where people, caught on hidden camera, in a blind taste test, chose Pepsi over rival Coca-Cola.

a. 28-hour day
b. 1990 Clean Air Act
c. 33 Strategies of War
d. Comparative advertising

6. _____ describes the relocation by a company of a business process from one country to another -- typically an operational process, such as manufacturing such as accounting. Even state governments employ _____.

The term is in use in several distinct but closely related ways.

a. A4e
b. A Stake in the Outcome
c. AAAI
d. Offshoring

7. _____ is subcontracting a process, such as product design or manufacturing, to a third-party company. The decision to outsource is often made in the interest of lowering cost or making better use of time and energy costs, redirecting or conserving energy directed at the competencies of a particular business, or to make more efficient use of land, labor, capital, (information) technology and resources. _____ became part of the business lexicon during the 1980s.

a. Outsourcing
b. Unemployment insurance
c. Operant conditioning
d. Opinion leadership

8. _____ is a contract between two parties, one being the employer and the other being the employee. An employee may be defined as: 'A person in the service of another under any contract of hire, express or implied, oral or written, where the employer has the power or right to control and direct the employee in the material details of how the work is to be performed.' Black's Law Dictionary page 471 (5th ed. 1979.)
a. Exit interview
b. Employment counsellor
c. Employment rate
d. Employment

9. _____ or contractualism is the freedom of individuals to bargain among themselves the terms of their own contracts, without government interference. Anything more than minimal regulations and taxes may be seen as infringements. It is the underpinning of the theory of laissez-faire economics.
a. Laissez-faire
b. Libertarian
c. Deep ecology
d. Freedom of contract

10. _____ is a concept in ethics with several meanings. It is often used synonymously with such concepts as responsibility, answerability, enforcement, blameworthiness, liability and other terms associated with the expectation of account-giving. As an aspect of governance, it has been central to discussions related to problems in both the public and private (corporation) worlds.
a. Usury
b. A4e
c. A Stake in the Outcome
d. Accountability

11. The _____ of 1990 (ADA) is the short title of United States (Pub.L. 101-336, 104 Stat. 327, enacted July 26, 1990), codified at 42 U.S.C. Â§ 12101 et seq. It was signed into law on July 26, 1990, by President George H. W. Bush, and later amended with changes effective January 1, 2009. The ADA is a wide-ranging civil rights law that prohibits, under certain circumstances, discrimination based on disability. It affords similar protections against discrimination to Americans with disabilities as the Civil Rights Act of 1964,

Chapter 17. The Changing Workplace

a. Equal Pay Act of 1963
b. Employment discrimination
c. Australian labour law
d. Americans with Disabilities Act

12. _____ is one of the managerial functions like planning, organizing, staffing and directing. It is an important function because it helps to check the errors and to take the corrective action so that deviation from standards are minimized and stated goals of the organization are achieved in desired manner. According to modern concepts, _____ is a foreseeing action whereas earlier concept of _____ was used only when errors were detected. _____ in management means setting standards, measuring actual performance and taking corrective action.
    a. Decision tree pruning
    b. Turnover
    c. Schedule of reinforcement
    d. Control

13. The U.S. _____ of 1988 ('_____') generally prevents employers from using lie detector tests, either for pre-employment screening or during the course of employment, with certain exemptions. Employers generally may not require or request any employee or job applicant to take a lie detector test, or discharge, discipline, or discriminate against an employee or job applicant for refusing to take a test or for exercising other rights under the Act. In addition, employers are required to display a poster in the workplace explaining the _____ for their employees.
    a. A Stake in the Outcome
    b. A4e
    c. Employee Polygraph Protection Act
    d. AAAI

14. The _____ is a United States labor law allowing an employee to take unpaid leave due to a serious health condition that makes the employee unable to perform his job or to care for a sick family member or to care for a new son or daughter (including by birth, adoption or foster care.) The bill was among the first signed into law by President Bill Clinton in his first term.
    a. Contributory negligence
    b. Family and Medical Leave Act of 1993
    c. Harvester Judgment
    d. Sarbanes-Oxley Act of 2002

15. _____ is the process of learning a new skill or trade, often in response to a change in the economic environment. Generally it reflects changes in profession choice rather than an 'upward' movement in the same field.

Chapter 17. The Changing Workplace

There is some controversy surrounding the use of _____ to offset economic changes caused by free trade and automation.

   a. Compliance Training
   b. Krauthammer
   c. Suspension training
   d. Retraining

16. The International Brotherhood of _____ is a labor union in the United States and Canada. Formed in 1903 by the merger of several local and regional locals of _____, the union now represents a diverse membership of blue-collar and professional workers in both the public and private sectors. The union had approximately 1.4 million members in 2007.
   a. 28-hour day
   b. 33 Strategies of War
   c. 1990 Clean Air Act
   d. Teamsters

17. _____ , which can be translated literally from Japanese as 'death from overwork', is occupational sudden death. Although this category has a significant count, Japan is one of the few countries that reports it in the statistics as a separate category. The major medical causes of _____ deaths are heart attack and stroke due to stress.
   a. 1990 Clean Air Act
   b. 33 Strategies of War
   c. Karoshi
   d. 28-hour day

18. _____ is a cross-disciplinary area concerned with protecting the safety, health and welfare of people engaged in work or employment. The goal of all _____ programs is to foster a work free safe environment. As a secondary effect, it may also protect co-workers, family members, employers, customers, suppliers, nearby communities, and other members of the public who are impacted by the workplace environment.
   a. A4e
   b. A Stake in the Outcome
   c. AAAI
   d. Occupational Safety and Health

Chapter 17. The Changing Workplace

19. The _____ is the primary federal law which governs occupational health and safety in the private sector and federal government in the United States. It was enacted by Congress in 1970 and was signed by President Richard Nixon on December 29, 1970. Its main goal is to ensure that employers provide employees with an environment free from recognized hazards, such as exposure to toxic chemicals, excessive noise levels, mechanical dangers, heat or cold stress, or unsanitary conditions.
    a. United States Department of Justice
    b. Unemployment and Farm Relief Act
    c. Unemployment Action Center
    d. Occupational Safety and Health Act

20. The _____ is a Cabinet department of the United States government responsible for occupational safety, wage and hour standards, unemployment insurance benefits, re-employment services, and some economic statistics. Many U.S. states also have such departments. The department is headed by the United States Secretary of Labor.
    a. AAAI
    b. A4e
    c. A Stake in the Outcome
    d. United States Department of Labor

21. _____ 489 U.S. 656 (1989) was a United States Supreme Court case involving the Fourth Amendment and its implication on drug testing programs. The majority of the court upheld the drug testing program in United States Customs Service.

In 1986, the U.S. Customs Service imposed a drug testing program for 'employees seeking transfer or promotion to positions having direct involvement in drug interdiction,' required to carry firearms, or have access to classified information.

   a. National Treasury Employees Union v. Von Raab
   b. NLRB v. J. Weingarten, Inc.
   c. Wards Cove Packing Co. v. Atonio
   d. Griggs v. Duke Power Co.

22. In employment law, a (BFOQ) (US) or bona fide occupational requirement (BFOR) (Canada) is a quality or an attribute that employers are allowed to consider when making decisions on the hiring and retention of employees - qualities that, when considered, in other contexts would be considered discriminatory and thus violating civil rights employment law.

Chapter 17. The Changing Workplace

In employment discrimination law in the United States, United States Code Title 29, Chapter 14 (age discrimination in employment), section 623 (prohibition of age discrimination) establishes that 'It shall not be unlawful for an employer, employment agency, or labor organization (1) to take any action otherwise prohibited under subsections (a), (b), (c), or (e) of this section where age is a _____ reasonably necessary to the normal operation of the particular business, or where the differentiation is based on reasonable factors other than age, or where such practices involve an employee in a workplace in a foreign country, and compliance with such subsections would cause such employer, or a corporation controlled by such employer, to violate the laws of the country in which such workplace is located.'

One example of _____s are mandatory retirement ages for bus drivers and airline pilots, for safety reasons. Further, in advertising, a manufacturer of men's clothing may lawfully advertise for male models.

   a. Bona fide occupational qualification
   b. Sick leave
   c. Corporate governance
   d. MacPherson v. Buick Motor Co.

23. The _____ was a landmark piece of legislation in the United States that outlawed racial segregation in schools, public places, and employment.
   a. Negligence in employment
   b. Civil Rights Act of 1964
   c. Financial Security Law of France
   d. Design patent

24. _____ a term coined in the mid-20th century, refers to the belief or attitude that one gender or sex is inferior to, less competent, or less valuable than the other. It can also refer to hatred of, or prejudice towards, either sex as a whole, or the application of stereotypes of masculinity in relation to men, or of femininity in relation to women. It is also called male and female chauvinism.
   a. Separate but equal
   b. Reverse discrimination
   c. 1990 Clean Air Act
   d. Sexism,

25. _____ is the self-government of a nation, country or some portion thereof, generally exercising sovereignty.

The term _____ is used in contrast to subjugation, which refers to a region as a 'territory' --subject to the political and military control of an external government. The word is sometimes used in a weaker sense to contrast with hegemony, the indirect control of one nation by another, more powerful nation.

a. A Stake in the Outcome
b. A4e
c. AAAI
d. Independence

26. _____ refers to discriminatory employment practices such as bias in hiring, promotion, job assignment, termination, and compensation, and various types of harassment.

In many countries, laws prohibit employers from discriminating on the basis of race, color, sex, religion, national origin, physical or mental disability, or age. There is also a growing body of law preventing or occasionally justifying _____ based on sexual orientation or gender identity.

a. Extra time
b. Employment discrimination
c. Invitee
d. Employee Retirement Income Security Act

27. The _____ was a United States federal law proposed by Republican Senator Charles Sumner and Republican Congressman Benjamin F. Butler in 1870. The act was passed by Congress in February, 1875 and signed by President Grant on March 1, 1875.

a. Civil Rights Act of 1875
b. Competition law
c. Negligence in employment
d. Diminishing returns

28. The term _____ was created by President Lyndon B. Johnson when he signed Executive Order 11246 on September 24, 1965, created to prohibit federal contractors from discriminating against employees on the basis of race, sex, creed, religion, color, or national origin. In more recent times, most employers have also added sexual orientation to the list of non-discrimination.

The Executive Order also required contractors to implement affirmative action plans to increase the participation of minorities and women in the workplace.

a. A Stake in the Outcome
b. A4e
c. AAAI
d. Equal Employment Opportunity

Chapter 17. The Changing Workplace

29. The U.S. _____ is a federal agency whose goal is ending employment discrimination. The _____ investigates discrimination complaints based on an individual's race, color, national origin, religion, sex, age, disability and retaliation for reporting and/or opposing a discriminatory practice. The Commission is also tasked with filing suits on behalf of alleged victim(s) of discrimination against employers and as an adjudicatory for claims of discrimination brought against federal agencies.
   a. ARCO
   b. Airbus SAS
   c. Airbus Industrie
   d. Equal Employment Opportunity Commission

30. In US employment law, _____ is defined as a substantially different rate of selection in hiring, promotion sex statistical significance tests, and/or practical significance tests. _____ is often used interchangeably with 'disparate impact,' which was a legal term coined in one of the most significant U.S. Supreme Court rulings on disparate or _____: Griggs v. Duke Power Co., 1971.
   a. AAAI
   b. Adverse impact
   c. A4e
   d. A Stake in the Outcome

31. A _____ is one scenario provided for evaluation by respondents in a Choice Experiment. Responses are collected and used to create a Choice Model. Respondents are usually provided with a series of differing _____s for evaluation.
   a. Thurstone scale
   b. Pairwise comparison
   c. Choice Set
   d. Computerized classification test

32.

The terms _____ and positive action refer to policies that take race, ethnicity, or gender into consideration in an attempt to promote equal opportunity. The focus of such policies ranges from employment and education to public contracting and health programs. The impetus towards _____ is twofold: to maximize diversity in all levels of society, along with its presumed benefits, and to redress perceived disadvantages due to overt, institutional, or involuntary discrimination.

a. Adam Smith
b. Affiliation
c. Abraham Harold Maslow
d. Affirmative action

33. _____, 443 U.S. 193 (1979), was a case regarding affirmative action in which the United States Supreme Court held that the Civil Rights Act of 1964 did not bar employers from favoring women and minorities. The Court's decision reversed lower courts' rulings in favor of Brian Weber whose lawsuit beginning in 1974 challenged his employer's hiring practices.

Brian Weber, a 32 year old laboratory analyst at a chemical plant, was excluded from a job training program that, if completed, would have significantly raised his pay.

a. AAAI
b. A Stake in the Outcome
c. United Steelworkers of America v. Weber
d. A4e

34. _____, 448 U.S. 448 (1980), was a case in which the United States Supreme Court held that the U.S. Congress could constitutionally use its spending power to remedy past discrimination. The case arose as a suit against the enforcement of provisions in a 1977 spending bill that required 10% of federal funds going towards public works programs to go to minority-owned companies.

The Court was deeply divided as to both the rationale for the decision and the outcome.

a. Griggs v. Duke Power Co.
b. NLRB v. J. Weingarten, Inc.
c. Fullilove v. Klutznick
d. Wards Cove Packing Co. v. Atonio

35. The _____ is a United States statute that was passed in response to a series of United States Supreme Court decisions which limited the rights of employees who had sued their employers for discrimination. The Act represented the first effort since the passage of the Civil Rights Act of 1964 to modify some of the basic procedural and substantive rights provided by federal law in employment discrimination cases. It provided for the right to trial by jury on discrimination claims and introduced the possibility of emotional distress damages, while limiting the amount that a jury could award

The 1991 Act combined elements from two different civil rights acts of the past: the Civil Rights Act of 1866, better known by the number assigned to it in the codification of federal laws as 'Section 1981', and the employment-related provisions of the Civil Rights Act of 1964, generally referred to as 'Title VII', its location within the Act.

a. Negligence in employment
b. Resource Conservation and Recovery Act
c. Covenant
d. Civil Rights Act of 1991

36. The _____ of 1967, Pub. L. No. 90-202, 81 Stat. 602 (Dec. 15, 1967), codified as Chapter 14 of Title 29 of the United States Code, 29 U.S.C. § 621 through 29 U.S.C. § 634 (ADEA), prohibits employment discrimination against persons 40 years of age or older in the United States). The law also sets standards for pensions and benefits provided by employers and requires that information about the needs of older workers be provided to the general public.
a. Extra time
b. Undue hardship
c. Unemployment and Farm Relief Act
d. Age Discrimination in Employment Act

37. The _____ 1970 is an Act of the United Kingdom Parliament which prohibits any less favourable treatment between men and women in terms of pay and conditions of employment. It came into force on 29 December 1975. The term pay is interpreted in a broad sense to include, on top of wages, things like holidays, pension rights, company perks and some kinds of bonuses.
a. Oncale v. Sundowner Offshore Services
b. Architectural Barriers Act of 1968
c. Equal Pay Act
d. Australian labour law

38. _____ occurs when expectant women are fired, not hired, or otherwise discriminated against due to their pregnancy or intention to become pregnant. Common forms of _____ include not being hired due to visible pregnancy or likelihood of becoming pregnant, being fired after informing an employer of one's pregnancy, being fired after maternity leave, and receiving a pay dock due to pregnancy. In the United States, since 1978, employers are legally bound to provide what insurance, leave pay, and additional support that would be bestowed upon any employee with medical leave or disability.
a. 28-hour day
b. 33 Strategies of War
c. 1990 Clean Air Act
d. Pregnancy Discrimination

39. _____ is the distribution of groups defined by ascribed characteristics, mostly gender, across occupations. More basically, it is the concentration of a similar group of people (be they males, females, whites, blacks, etc) in a job. _____ levels differ on a basis of perfect segregation and integration.

a. AAAI
b. A4e
c. A Stake in the Outcome
d. Occupational segregation

40. In economics, the term _____ refers to situations where the advancement of a qualified person within the hierarchy of an organization is stopped at a lower level because of some form of discrimination, most commonly sexism or racism, but since the term was coined, '_____' has also come to describe the limited advancement of the deaf, blind, disabled, aged and sexual minorities. It is an unofficial, invisible barrier that prevents women and minorities from advancing in businesses.

This situation is referred to as a 'ceiling' as there is a limitation blocking upward advancement, and 'glass' (transparent) because the limitation is not immediately apparent and is normally an unwritten and unofficial policy. This invisible barrier continues to exist, even though there are no explicit obstacles keeping minorities from acquiring advanced job positions - there are no advertisements that specifically say 'no minorities hired at this establishment', nor are there any formal orders that say 'minorities are not qualified' - but they do lie beneath the surface.

a. 33 Strategies of War
b. 28-hour day
c. 1990 Clean Air Act
d. Glass ceiling

41. _____ indicates a more-or-less equal exchange or substitution of goods or services. English speakers often use the term to mean 'a favour for a favour' and the phrases with almost identical meaning include: 'what for what,' 'give and take,' 'tit for tat', 'this for that', and 'you scratch my back, and I'll scratch yours'.

In legal usage, _____ indicates that an item or a service has been traded in return for something of value, usually when the propriety or equity of the transaction is in question.

a. Quid pro quo
b. 33 Strategies of War
c. 1990 Clean Air Act
d. 28-hour day

42. _____ is unwelcome harassment of a sexual nature, or based upon the receiving party's sex or gender. In some contexts or circumstances, _____ may be illegal. It includes a range of behavior from seemingly mild transgressions and annoyances to actual sexual abuse or sexual assault.

a. 1990 Clean Air Act
b. 28-hour day
c. Hypernorms
d. Sexual harassment

43. The 'business case for _____', theorizes that in a global marketplace, a company that employs a diverse workforce (both men and women, people of many generations, people from ethnically and racially diverse backgrounds etc.) is better able to understand the demographics of the marketplace it serves and is thus better equipped to thrive in that marketplace than a company that has a more limited range of employee demographics.

An additional corollary suggests that a company that supports the _____ of its workforce can also improve employee satisfaction, productivity and retention.

a. Trademark
b. Diversity
c. Virtual team
d. Kanban

44. The _____ (Situation, Task, Action, Result) format is a job interview technique used by interviewers to gather all the relevant information about a specific capability that the job requires. This interview format is said to have a higher degree of predictability of future on-the-job performance than the traditional interview.

- Situation: The interviewer wants you to present a recent challenge and situation in which you found yourself.
- Task: What did you have to achieve? The interviewer will be looking to see what you were trying to achieve from the situation.
- Action: What did you do? The interviewer will be looking for information on what you did, why you did it and what were the alternatives.
- Results: What was the outcome of your actions? What did you achieve through your actions and did you meet your objectives. What did you learn from this experience and have you used this learning since?

a. Rasch models
b. Competency-based job descriptions
c. Phrase completion
d. Star

1. _____ is the set of processes, customs, policies, laws, and institutions affecting the way a corporation (or company) is directed, administered or controlled. _____ also includes the relationships among the many stakeholders involved and the goals for which the corporation is governed. The principal stakeholders are the shareholders/members, management, and the board of directors.
   a. No-FEAR Act
   b. Flextime
   c. Corporate governance
   d. Guarantee

2. The _____ is a private, not-for-profit organization whose primary purpose is to develop generally accepted accounting principles (GAAP) within the United States in the public's interest. The Securities and Exchange Commission (SEC) designated the _____ as the organization responsible for setting accounting standards for public companies in the U.S. It was created in 1973, replacing the Committee on Accounting Procedure (CAP) and the Accounting Principles Board (APB) of the American Institute of Certified Public Accountants (AICPA.)

The _____'s mission is 'to establish and improve standards of financial accounting and reporting for the guidance and education of the public, including issuers, auditors, and users of financial information.' To achieve this, _____ has five goals:

- Improve the usefulness of financial reporting by focusing on the primary characteristics of relevance and reliability, and on the qualities of comparability and consistency.
- Keep standards current to reflect changes in methods of doing business and in the economy.
- Consider promptly any significant areas of deficiency in financial reporting that might be improved through standard setting.
- Promote international convergence of accounting standards concurrent with improving the quality of financial reporting.
- Improve common understanding of the nature and purposes of information in financial reports.

The _____ is not a governmental body. The SEC has legal authority to establish financial accounting and reporting standards for publicly held companies under the Securities Exchange Act of 1934.

   a. Chief risk officer
   b. Foreign direct investment
   c. Prospero Business Suite
   d. Financial Accounting Standards Board

3. The _____ of 2002 (Pub.L. 107-204, 116 Stat. 745, enacted July 30, 2002), also known as the Public Company Accounting Reform and Investor Protection Act of 2002 and commonly called Sarbanes-Oxley, Sarbox or SOX, is a United States federal law enacted on July 30, 2002, as a reaction to a number of major corporate and accounting scandals including those affecting Enron, Tyco International, Adelphia, Peregrine Systems and WorldCom.

a. Fair Labor Standards Act
b. Sarbanes-Oxley Act of 2002
c. Letter of credit
d. Sarbanes-Oxley Act

4. An _____ is any party that makes an investment.

The term has taken on a specific meaning in finance to describe the particular types of people and companies that regularly purchase equity or debt securities for financial gain in exchange for funding an expanding company. Less frequently, the term is applied to parties who purchase real estate, currency, commodity derivatives, personal property, or other assets.

a. AAAI
b. Investor
c. A Stake in the Outcome
d. A4e

5. The U.S. _____ is an independent agency of the United States government which holds primary responsibility for enforcing the federal securities laws and regulating the securities industry, the nation's stock and options exchanges, and other electronic securities markets. The SEC was created by section 4 of the Securities Exchange Act of 1934 (now codified as 15 U.S.C. Â§ 78d and commonly referred to as the 1934 Act.)

a. 1990 Clean Air Act
b. Securities and Exchange Commission
c. 33 Strategies of War
d. 28-hour day

6. _____ is a worldwide management consulting firm that focuses on solving issues of concern to senior management. McKinsey serves as an advisor to the world's leading businesses, governments, and institutions. It is widely recognized as a leader and one of the most prestigious firms in the management consulting industry.

a. 33 Strategies of War
b. 28-hour day
c. McKinsey ' Company
d. 1990 Clean Air Act

7. The _____ is an independent, not-for-profit membership organization, dedicated to serving the corporate governance needs of directors of public, private, and non-profit organizations. Founded in 1977, NACD is headquartered in Washington, D.C. and serves approximately 10,000 members. NACD's stated mission is to achieve improved corporate performance through better board practice.

a. Goodyear Tire ' Rubber
b. Business Roundtable
c. Financial Accounting Standards Board
d. National Association of Corporate Directors

8. _____ of corporations are a central part of corporate law and corporate governance and describe which obligations people owe to companies by virtue of their position as directors. Because directors exercise control and management over the company, but companies are run (in theory at least) for the benefit of the shareholders, the law imposes strict duties on directors in relation to the exercise of their duties. The duties imposed upon directors are fiduciary duties, similar in nature to those that the law imposes on those in similar positions of trust: agents and trustees.

a. Duties of directors
b. Rasch models
c. Linear regression
d. Structure follows strategy

9. _____ are organizations which pool large sums of money and invest those sums in companies. They include banks, insurance companies, retirement or pension funds, hedge funds and mutual funds. Their role in the economy is to act as highly specialized investors on behalf of others.

a. A Stake in the Outcome
b. A4e
c. AAAI
d. Institutional investors

10. A mutual _____ or stockholder is an individual or company (including a corporation) that legally owns one or more shares of stock in a joint stock company. A company's _____s collectively own that company. Thus, the typical goal of such companies is to enhance _____ value.

a. Free riding
b. 1990 Clean Air Act
c. Stockholder
d. Shareholder

11. A chief executive officer (_____) or chief executive is one of the highest-ranking corporate officer (executive) or administrator in charge of total management. An individual selected as President and _____ of a corporation, company, organization, or agency, reports to the board of directors. In internal communication and press releases, many companies capitalize the term and those of other high positions, even when they are not proper nouns.

a. Chief executive officer
b. Director of communications
c. CEO
d. Portfolio manager

12. In finance, an _____ is a contract between a buyer and a seller that gives the buyer the right--but not the obligation-- to buy or to sell a particular asset (the underlying asset) at a later day at an agreed price. In return for granting the _____, the seller collects a payment (the premium) from the buyer. A call _____ gives the buyer the right to buy the underlying asset; a put _____ gives the buyer of the _____ the right to sell the underlying asset.
   a. Option
   b. A Stake in the Outcome
   c. AAAI
   d. A4e

13. While the full name of the Swiss verein is Deloitte Touche Tohmatsu, in 1989 it initially branded itself _____ and then simply Deloitte. In 2003 the rebranding campaign was commissioned by Bill Parrett, the then CEO of DTT, and led by Jerry Leamon, the global Clients and Markets leader.

Deloitte member firms offer services in the following functions, with country-specific variations on their legal implementation (i.e. all operating within a single company or through separate legal entities operating as subsidiaries of an umbrella legal entity for the country.)

   a. 33 Strategies of War
   b. 28-hour day
   c. 1990 Clean Air Act
   d. Deloitte ' Touche

ANSWER KEY

Chapter 1
1. c   2. d   3. c   4. b   5. a   6. a

Chapter 2
1. d   2. c   3. b   4. d   5. d   6. d   7. b   8. b

Chapter 3
1. d   2. c   3. d   4. d   5. d   6. b

Chapter 4
1. d   2. a   3. d   4. d   5. a   6. a   7. d   8. a   9. c   10. b
11. d   12. c   13. b   14. c   15. d   16. a   17. c

Chapter 5
1. d   2. b   3. a   4. c   5. d   6. a   7. b   8. d   9. d   10. d
11. b   12. b   13. b   14. a   15. b

Chapter 6
1. b   2. a   3. d   4. b   5. c   6. c   7. d   8. d   9. d   10. d
11. c   12. b   13. a   14. a

Chapter 7
1. d   2. d   3. d   4. d   5. d   6. d   7. d   8. b   9. d   10. b
11. a   12. b

Chapter 8
1. d   2. d   3. d   4. b   5. d   6. b

Chapter 9
1. b   2. c   3. a   4. c   5. d   6. d   7. c   8. a   9. d   10. d
11. c

Chapter 10
1. b   2. d   3. c   4. d   5. d   6. d   7. a   8. d   9. c   10. b
11. d   12. d   13. d   14. d   15. a   16. a   17. d   18. a   19. d   20. d
21. a   22. d   23. d   24. d

Chapter 11
1. d   2. d   3. d   4. d   5. c   6. d   7. c   8. b   9. c   10. b
11. d   12. a   13. d   14. d   15. d   16. d   17. c   18. c   19. d   20. d

Chapter 12
1. c   2. a   3. c   4. b   5. d   6. d   7. d   8. c   9. b   10. c
11. b   12. c   13. c   14. a

Chapter 13
1. b   2. d   3. d   4. c   5. d   6. b   7. d   8. b   9. c   10. c
11. c   12. b

Chapter 14
1. d   2. b   3. a   4. d   5. a   6. d   7. b   8. d   9. d   10. c
11. c   12. a   13. c

Chapter 15
1. d   2. a   3. d   4. d   5. d   6. d   7. d   8. d   9. c   10. d
11. a   12. d   13. d   14. b

Chapter 16
1. c   2. b   3. c   4. b   5. d   6. d   7. a   8. d   9. d   10. a
11. c   12. a   13. d   14. d   15. d   16. a   17. d   18. d   19. c   20. d
21. a   22. d   23. c   24. a

Chapter 17
1. a   2. d   3. d   4. c   5. d   6. d   7. a   8. d   9. d   10. d
11. d   12. d   13. c   14. b   15. d   16. d   17. c   18. d   19. d   20. d
21. a   22. a   23. b   24. d   25. d   26. b   27. a   28. d   29. d   30. b
31. c   32. d   33. c   34. c   35. d   36. d   37. c   38. d   39. d   40. d
41. a   42. d   43. b   44. d

Chapter 18
1. c   2. d   3. d   4. b   5. b   6. c   7. d   8. a   9. d   10. d
11. c   12. a   13. d

www.ingramcontent.com/pod-product-compliance
Lightning Source LLC
Chambersburg PA
CBHW081847230426
43669CB00018B/2859